Whittling Ideas for Beginners

Whittling Made Easy for Beginners, Including Step by Step Whittling Project Ideas for Beginners for Every Season

Introduction

Have you come across a wooden sculpture that picked your fancy? Would you like to become a seasoned carpenter or wooden sculptor? Are you interested in picking whittling as your newfound hobby?

If so, then keep reading.

The art of whittling traces its roots back to the early man when he used to carve things for his survival. This form of art has evolved over the years and has seen the creation of beautiful masterpieces over the past centuries. A good example is the Chinese wooden Bodhisattva at the Shanghai Museum, Jin dynasty (1115-1234).

Over the years, wood carving has undergone many changes and has kept on getting better and better. Whittling is an art that allows you to express yourself through art as you reconnect with nature and our ancestors.

Perhaps you're wondering...

Is it possible to sculpt amazing images even if you've never whittled before?

- Yes, with the right tools and guidelines, you'll be able to carve any kind of image.

What do you need to become a whittler?

- A whittling knife and protective gear are all you need to get started on whittling.

Can you make a living from whittling?

- Yes, it is possible to make a living as a professional whittler. Once you master this art and create great pieces of art, you'll be able to sell them to people and make an income.

If you have such questions and any other related questions, this will be discussed in this book. Not only does this elaborate guide offer you all you need to know about how to get started on whittling, but it also offers you amazing whittling projects for you to get started.

Let's jump right in!

Table of Contents

Introduction ______ **2**

Chapter 1: How to Get Started On Whittling 6

Wood ______ 6

Technique ______ 7

Whittling tools ______ 8

Some Whittling Pointers on How to Whittle Wood ______ 9

Essential Whittling Tips For Beginners ______ 10

Chapter 2: Whittling Project Ideas for Beginners- For Every Season ______ **12**

Utensils Whittling Projects ______ 12

Whittling Animal Projects ______ 34

Carving Little People ______ 96

Other Whittling Projects ______ 121

Conclusion ______ **153**

Chapter 1: How to Get Started On Whittling

Before you can start on your first project, you must learn the fundamental aspects of whittling to help you be successful in doing the projects we are going to discuss later on.

However, we will not discuss them in depth because more details are well explained in the previous series of this book, *Whittling Guide For Beginners.*

The first thing we are going to look at is the wood you are going to use.

Wood

When it comes to whittling, you can use pretty much any type of wood. Some of the most common softwoods include;

- Basswood
- Pine
- Balsa

This softwood is perfect because it won't be too hard to cut through, and it's also straight grains.

Furthermore, pine is excellent because it is readily available; you can even find lots of it in your backyard.

Technique

Another critical aspect when it comes to whittling is the technique. You can use various ways to shape a piece of wood with your knife, but there are only 3 main ways to efficiently and adequately carve a piece of wood. These cutting techniques include straightforward rough cuts, push stroke, and pull stroke or pare cut.

1. Straightaway Rough Cut

This is the cut you begin with when starting off your project. It helps to create the general shape of your project. To make this cut, you need to hold the wood with your left hand and the whittling knife firmly with your right hand. Make a long sweeping cut with the grain and away from you. Slice the wood severally to your desired shape or size. Make sure not to cut too deep to avoid splitting the wood.

2. Pull Stroke or Pare Cut

The pare cut or pull stroke is great because it gives you more control over the blade, and it is best suited for detailed cuts.

To make this cut, hold the wood using your left hand and hold your whittling knife firmly with your right hand. Now brace your right thumb against the wood, then squeeze your right finger to draw the whittling blade to your right thumb. Make sure to keep your thumb from the blade's path and keep your strokes short and controlled.

3. Push Stroke

The push stroke, just like the pull stroke, is perfect for detailed cuts and gives you more control over the blade.

Hold the wood using your left hand and the whittling knife firmly with your right hand facing away from you to make this cut. Now place both your left and right thumb on the back of the whittling blade. Push the blade into the wood using your left thumb while you guide the blade using your right thumb and fingers.

Whittling tools

The art of whittling is about the wood you use as much as it is the tools used to craft the wood. There are several whittling knives available, each with a specific use. You can read more on the different kinds of whittling knives best suited for you in the previous series, *Whittling Guide For Beginners*.

Another key tool to any whittler is the thumb guard, which protects your thumb from the sharp blade. You might also need a strong glove to help protect your arm as you whittle.

Some Whittling Pointers on How to Whittle Wood

When you decide to start whittling wood, you will need some basic techniques to get the job done. Here are some of the main tips to keep in mind when getting started on whittling.

1. Choose the Right Wood

The first thing to consider before you can start carving is to choose the right wood for the projects. Ensure that the wood you use is softwood, and pay attention to the wood grain. You should work with wood with straight wood grains because they are much easier to cut without chipping away. Some of the whittler's favorite woods include basswood, butternut, and balsa; you cannot go wrong with these.

2. Always Use a Whittling Knife

While you might be tempted to use any knife, most likely a pocket knife, and you can, it is always advisable to use a whittling knife. This is because whittling knives are designed in a good way such that they are sharper, more comfortable, and more reliable than other knives. However, if you decide to use a pocket knife, make sure you use the traditional knife, but the experience won't be the same as using a specialty whittling knife.

3. How to Cut the Wood

Once you've selected the wood and the tools you are going to use, another key aspect you need to keep in mind is how you will cut the wood. Always make sure that you cut and carve in the direction of the wood grain and not against it. This will help make it a lot easier for you to cut and carve through the wood. Additionally, use your thumb as the focal point so that it offers you the necessary force for you to whittle with precision.

4. Always Keep Your Whittling Blades Sharp

The first and foremost rule that any whittler should keep in mind is that your whittling knife should always be sharp at all times. Before and after using any blade, you should make sure that you sharpen your knife properly using a sharpening stone or a fine grit of around 320.

Essential Whittling Tips For Beginners

To help make sure that you have a smooth and easy time, here are some of the most important and quick tips to help make the most out of your whittling time.

1. For a beginner, never use hardwood like mahogany because they are challenging to work with. Always

make sure that you use softwood like basswood until you become a pro.

2. Make sure that while whittling, you use a blade of not more than 1.5 inches. This is to help you have more control over your whittling since your arm will be close to the material.

3. Before you can start whittling, draw a pattern or design using a #2 pencil to have a guideline for your project.

4. The slides you use should be comfortable and not too big. Work with slides of around 4 inches in size and not more.

5. Once you begin the whittling process, go slow and in small steps. Remember that you cannot go back once you make a cut; therefore, it is vital to have the plan in mind and go slowly to avoid making a mistake.

With all that in mind, you are ready to begin working on the various projects available for you to try.

Chapter 2: Whittling Project Ideas for Beginners- For Every Season

There is a huge selection of projects for you to try out as a beginner categorized into various groups such as animals, cars, and many more. The best part about these projects is that they are straightforward, such that you can be able to do them without any difficulty. Let's start with utensils you can carve out.

Utensils Whittling Projects

Spoon Carving

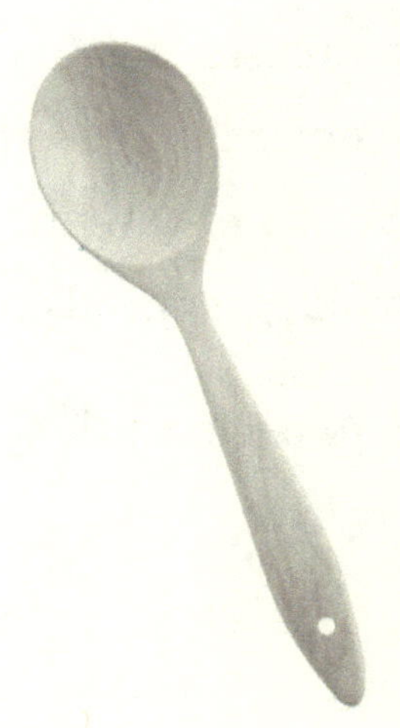

Whittling a spoon is a great activity that any whittler should try. This is because the process of carving is quite direct and easy. Also, having a spoon is quite beneficial for anyone.

The Required Materials

- A chunk of softwood that is a little bigger than the size of the spoon you intend to whittle.
- Small diameter sanding drum
- Grit sandpaper
- Food safe wood finish

Required tools

- Table saw
- Scroll saw
- Belt sander
- Dremmel tool

Procedure

1. Start by drawing the rough outline of the spoon that you'd like to whittle on the piece of wood.

2. The next thing is to cut the blank using the table saw or your whittling knife. You can also use a miter saw to cut the chunk of wood to the appropriate length.

3. Now you can use a scroll saw to cut along your outline, which you can comfortably do using your whittling knife.

4. Smooth out the edges of your spoon using your carving knife to give it the shape of a spoon.

5. Once you finish roughing out the handle, start rounding off the head of the spoon.

6. On the concave side of the spoon, use a hook knife or rounded sweep gouge to remove the materials.

7. Finish by sanding the spoon properly, then add the protective finish.

Hand-Carved Butter Knife

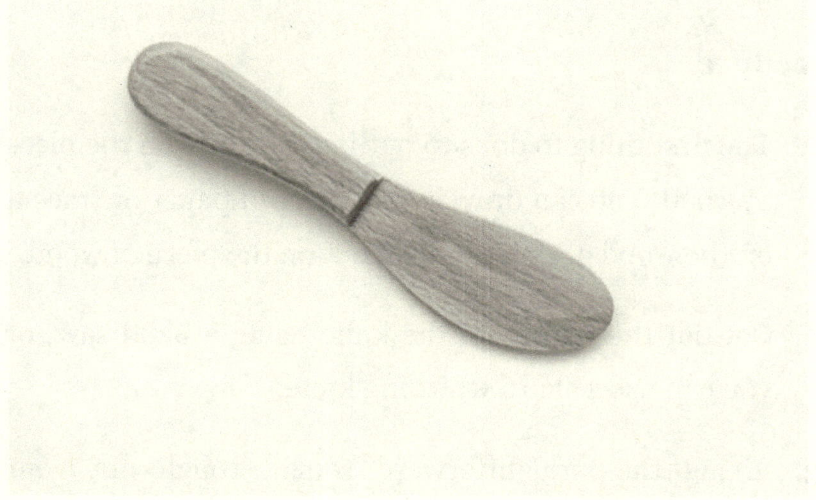

Another quite handy tool that we all need in our kitchen is a butter knife. You can use this knife to apply butter, margarine, or jam to your bread during breakfast. Additionally, it can be used to cut the soft things in your house.

The Required Materials

- A piece of softwood like Oakwood that is about 15 x 4 cm
- Sanding paper
- A whittling knife
- Band saw

- Pen
- Wood wax

Procedure

1. The first thing to do is to outline the knife on the piece of wood. You can draw it on a piece of paper or trace it on the wood or directly sketch it on the piece of wood.
2. Cut out the outline of the knife using a band saw, or you can use a sharp whittling knife.
3. Using the straightforward rough, rough out your knife. Make sure that you remove all the unnecessary wood until it resembles a knife.
4. Using the sandpaper, sand out every part of your knife, and once you're done, make your knife wet and sand once again.
5. Once your knife is all smooth, apply the beeswax to finish off your carving.

Wooden Fork

Like the spoon, a fork is usually an essential utensil for eating some foods. Therefore, making your own fork is a great project for you to try. Not only is it easy but also quite direct that any person can create.

The Required Materials

- A piece of wood that is roughly a bit bigger than the fork you intend to create
- A table saw
- Sandpaper
- A whittling knife
- A food-safe wood finish

Procedure

1. Start by tracing the outline of the fork on the piece of wood. Make sure that you mark distinctively.
2. Cut out the outline of the fork using a table saw or your whittling knife.
3. Now smooth and detail your blank using your whittling knife. Remove all the unnecessary wood until the blank is smooth and well detailed.
4. Use the hand saw to create the sharp points of the fork. Make sure that they are evenly spaced and equal in size.
5. Sand the fork thoroughly until it's smooth and well carved.

6. Finally, apply the food-safe wood finish.

Travel Fork-Spoon

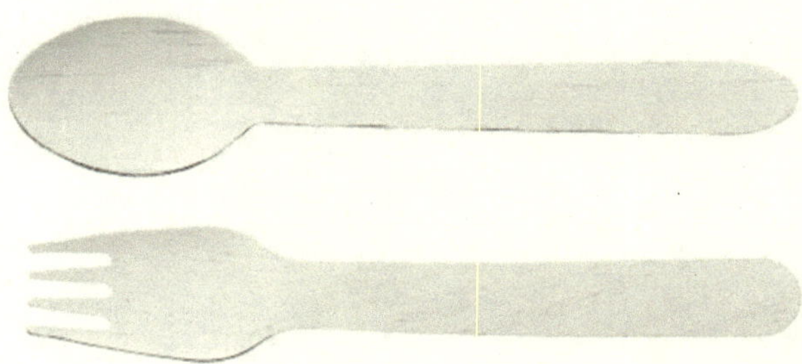

What do you think of the idea of a portable utensil? Well, this project is a great idea because it incorporates two essential tools into one. It is also quite easy and direct to create.

The Required Materials

- Table saw
- A piece of wood that is a bit bigger than the size of your project
- A sandpaper
- Small diameter sanding drum
- Pen
- A whittling knife

Procedure

1. Start by choosing how long the handle will be, based on what is comfortable for you. Mark a V-shaped groove to mark where the shaft begins and where the handle ends.

2. Now flatten the shaft by trimming down the top and bottom parts using the straightforward rough cuts.

3. Sharpen the tip of the shaft before making the prongs.

4. Make V grooves and continue shaping the fork to the proper shape and size. On the other side of the fork, use the gouge to make a hollow shape for the spoon.

5. Finally, sand the fork and add the food-safe wood finish.

Whittling a Wooden Spatula

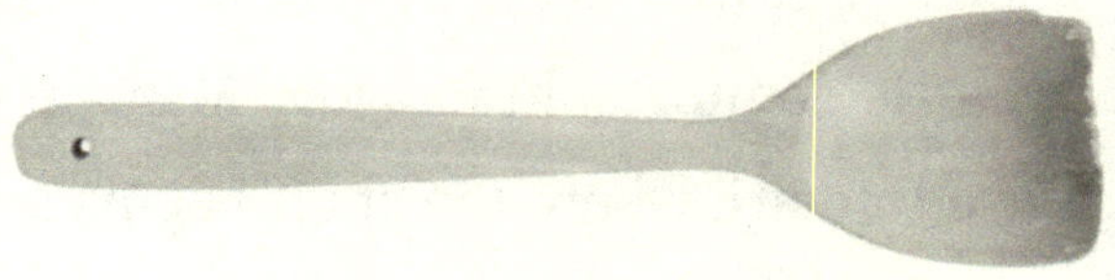

A spatula is a handy tool used in the kitchen, and everyone should have one. It helps when cooking foods such as pancakes, eggs, and most of the foods you cook on your pan. The best part is that it is effortless to create.

The Required Materials

- Wood carving knife
- Sweep gauge
- Sandpaper
- Food safe wood finish
- 9 inch Shinto saw rasp
- Beeswax butter

Procedure

1. Begin by selecting the wood you will use, then transfer the spatula's design to the piece of wood.

2. Use a jigsaw to cut out your design. Make sure to cut outside the edges of your mark.

3. Using your whittling knife, detail your spatula and remove the unwanted wood before using the gouge to work on the spatula's blade.

4. Now sand the spatula thoroughly until it's smooth before applying the wood finish.

Wooden Coffee Scoop

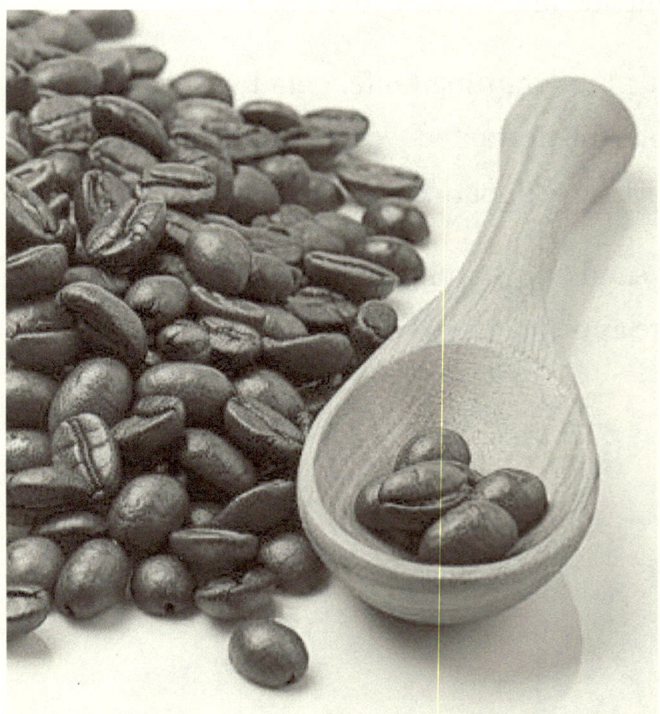

Having a spoon that you can use to scoop your coffee is great because you'll have a tool specially designed for that purpose. This removes the hustle of having to use different spoons when making your coffee. Moreover, it is easy to make and does not take a lot of time.

The Required Materials

- Straight blade whittling knife
- Jigsaw

- Carving gouge
- Hook knife
- Wood safe mineral oil
- Sandpaper

Procedure

1. Start by picking out the hardwoods with a closed-grain such as maple, birch, or walnut. Trace the shape of the scoop using a pencil on the piece of wood.
2. Now create the scoop body using the carving gouge until you get a good enough scoop area. Use your whittling knife to detail the back of the scoop to create a well-rounded backside.
3. Next, carve out the handle of your scoop by removing the unnecessary wood, then detail it to be smooth and straight. Make sure that the grip is comfortable for you.
4. Sand the whole coffee scoop thoroughly before adding the wood-safe mineral oil to the surface.

An Oven Push/Pull Stick

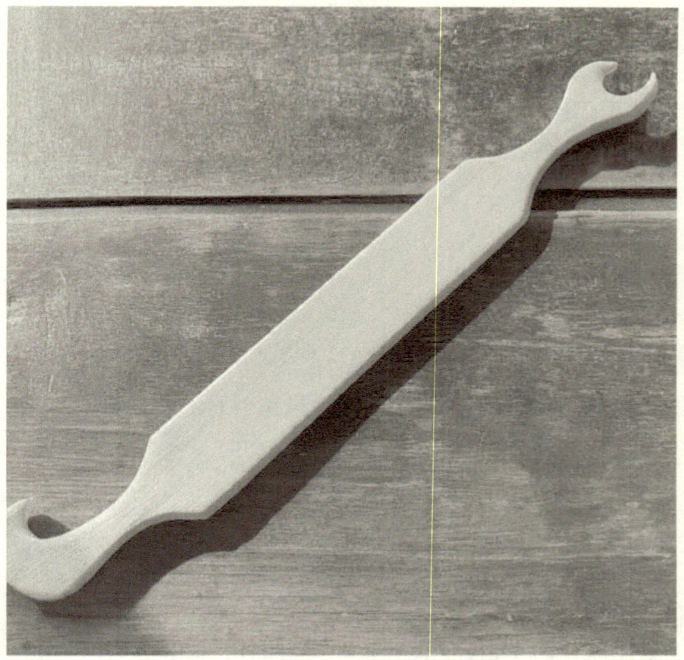

We usually use oven mitts to remove the oven rack, but sometimes the gloves may get burned or might not offer the best protection. That's why you'll need this push/pull stick to remove or return the rack when you're baking or cooking. The good thing is that it does not require much work for you to whittle.

The Required Materials

- Whittling knife
- A sandpaper

- Wood safe mineral oil
- Jigsaw or coping saw

Procedure

1. Begin by selecting the piece of wood you're going to use, most preferably softwood that you can easily work with.
2. Next, select the design for the push/pull stick, then trace it on the piece of wood you select.
3. Now cut it out using the jigsaw or tabletop band saw following the outline you've drawn.
4. Drill a hole at the end of the handle of your stick, then attach a leather strap to hang your stick.
5. Next, thoroughly sand your whole push/pull stick using the sandpaper, then apply the wood-safe mineral oil to finish it.

Wooden Honey Dipper

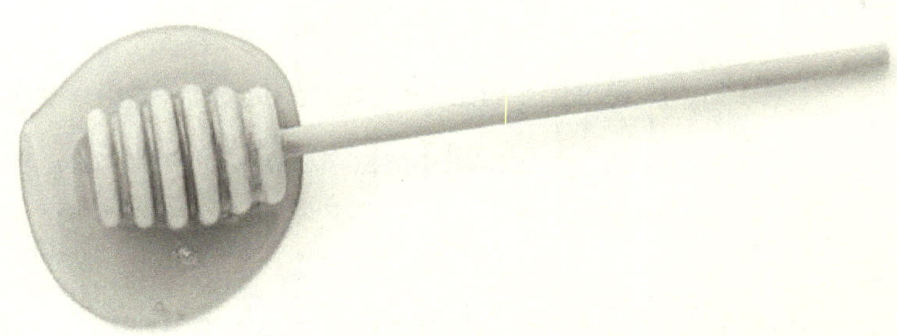

This wooden honey dipper can be handy, especially when having breakfast. You can use it to apply honey, jam, and any viscous liquid to your bread or food. It helps to remove the hustle of extracting these liquids. Moreover, making the dipper is relatively easy and does not require a lot of materials.

The Required Materials

- Jet mini-lathe
- A whittling knife
- Sandpaper
- Food safe mineral oil

Procedure

1. Start by choosing and preparing the wood for the dipper. Now trace the shape of the dipper on the piece of wood before cutting it out.

2. Next, use your whittling knife to cut the design out and round the blank into a cylindrical profile. You can, however, use a roughing gouge or a spindle gouge to round it up.

3. Make the honey dipper section by carving out the groves probably ¼ inch deep and spaced about ¼ inch or less apart.

4. Use the spindle gouge to shape the handle of the dipper.

5. Sand the honey dipper using the sandpaper before applying wood-safe mineral oil.

Making a Cutting Board

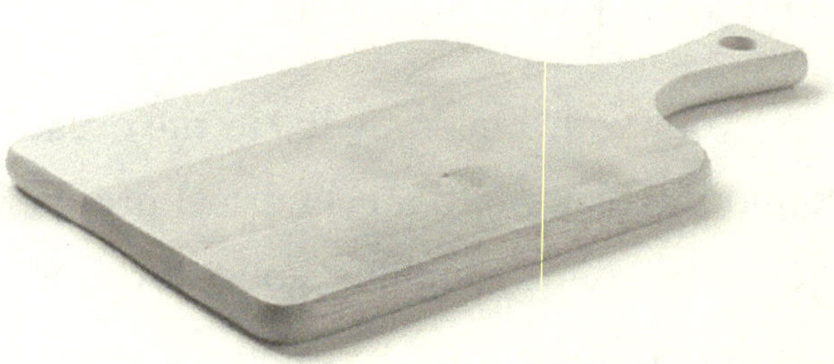

Having a cutting board in your home is essential because it helps you cut things in your kitchen. Instead of cutting your onions or tomatoes with your hand, which might lead to cuts and bruises, you can use this cutting board instead. It is quite easy to make and does not require a lot of things.

The Required Materials

- Table saw
- Parallel clamps
- Black and decker belt sander
- Sandpaper
- T square

- Wood such as maple, walnut, and cherry
- Food safe mineral oil

Procedure

1. Begin by choosing the dimensions of the cutting board by referring to other chopping boards you have. You can also decide to use these dimensions: 21 inches long, 9 inches wide, and 1.5 inches thick.
2. Sketch the dimensions on the piece of wood, then use your table saw to cut out the board along the outline you've drawn. You can use your whittling knife to shape or cut your cutting board.
3. If you decide to make a cutting board with different types of wood, arrange them simultaneously, then use glue to combine them before cutting them to size.
4. Use the sandpaper for sanding the whole board and router the edges to give it a rounded finish.
5. Finish by applying the food-safe mineral oil on the board.

Wooden Bowl

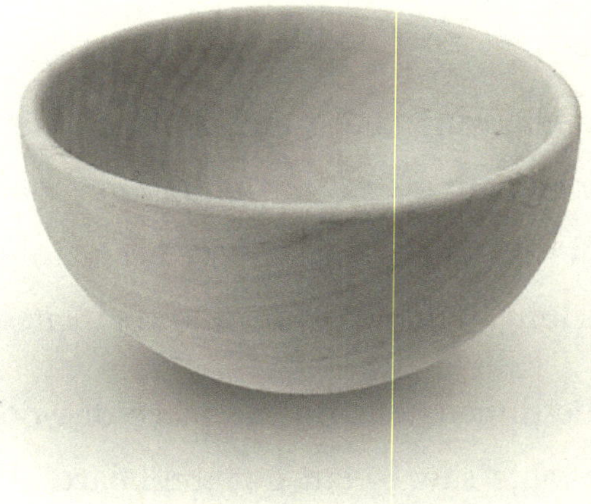

If you have a fork and a spoon already, then what's missing is a bowl to eat from. Indeed, it is possible to create your bowl out of nothing other than a whittling knife and wood.

This is quite essential, especially if you are camping and you need utensils to eat and don't have any. Moreover, it is also a good idea to have a bowl that fits your desired specifications. The best part is that it is not hard to carve a bowl.

The Required Materials

- A whittling knife
- A log of wood
- Hatchet

- Sandpaper
- Carved adze tool

Procedure

1. Start by outlining the bowl on the piece of wood, then use your whittling knife to cut the blank for the bowl.
2. Using the adze tool, make downward cutting motions to remove the large portions of wood. Continue doing this until you create a bowl-like shape.
3. Ensure that the wood is secured to your work surface, and use push cuts with your carving knife. Carve the outside of the bowl properly. Make sure that you don't punch through the walls of your bowl and keep checking the thickness of the bowl.
4. Continue carving with your knife until it assumes the shape of a bowl.
5. Using the sandpaper, sand the wholesale bowl thoroughly to remove all the uneven edges.
6. Finish by adding the food-safe mineral oil.

Whittling Animal Projects

Whittling a 5-Minute Owl

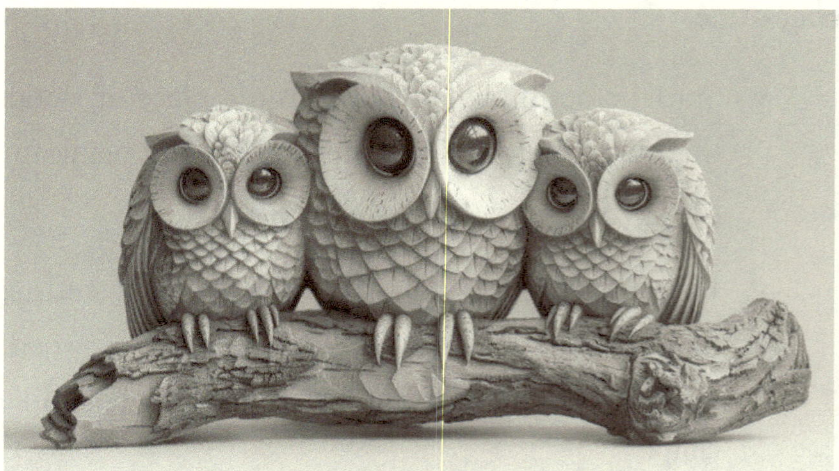

This project is a great idea for anyone looking to have a great ornament in their home. It is also a great project that builds confidence and teaches you all the fundamental carving techniques. The owl is easy for any beginner to create and includes all the basic cuts, i.e., push cuts, paring cuts, stop cuts, chip cuts, and stab cuts.

The Required Materials

- 1" by 1" by 6" basswood
- Carving knife
- Pencil

- Ruler
- ¼ inch #6 gouge
- Food safe mineral oil

Procedure

5. Start by drawing the top of the head. Do this by measuring ½" on the front, and back corners, then sketch a line from the side corners down to these marks. The two opposite sides of the blank will have two triangles.
6. Proceed to shape the top of the head using push cuts or pairing cuts. You want to remove the triangles that you sketched in the previous step until you form the top of the owl's head.
7. Draw the bottom of the head and body, then mark ⅛" deep stop cuts along these lines.
8. Use pairing cuts to rough out the owl's belly, between the perch and the bottom of the head to the stop cuts.
9. Sketch in the ears and beak before then use your knife to cut them out.
10. Make cuts on the perch to define the claws, then make two slight angled cuts above the eyes as eyebrows.

11. Add in the wings and the feathers using ⅙" #6 gouge to make stab cuts.

Whittling a Bear

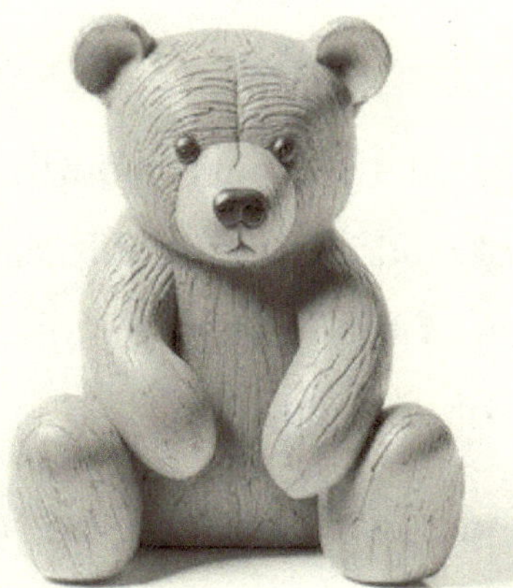

A whittled bear is considered one of the best art pieces one can own. They form a good image that adds a nice touch to any home, and they can also be a great souvenir to carry around. Whittling a bear is not as hard as many people might think. This is how you do it.

The Required Materials

- A whittling knife
- 16mm gouge
- ¼" gouge
- A pen

- A wood safe mineral oil
- Basswood

Procedure

1. Start by sketching out the general outline of the bear on the piece of wood you intend to carve. You can choose the size of the bear you want to make by varying the size of the wood.
2. You can use a band saw to cut out the front and side profile of the bear to get rid of the excess wood.
3. Using your whittling knife, make stop cuts along both legs to remove the excess wood.
4. Side profile your bear using a no 2 16mm gouge, then block in the face using the roughing knife.
5. Use your roughing knife to remove all the excess wood in your bear. Switch to a detailing knife, then shape the bear's head, body, arms, and legs.
6. Use a no 5 ¼" gouge to shape the eye mounds and a micro gouge to shape the nose and nostrils.

7. Use the no 5 ¼" to shape out the ears, and using the micro gouge, make shallow horizontal cuts around the bear's body to simulate the look of fur.

8. Finally, apply the wood-safe clear finish on your bear.

Making An Elephant

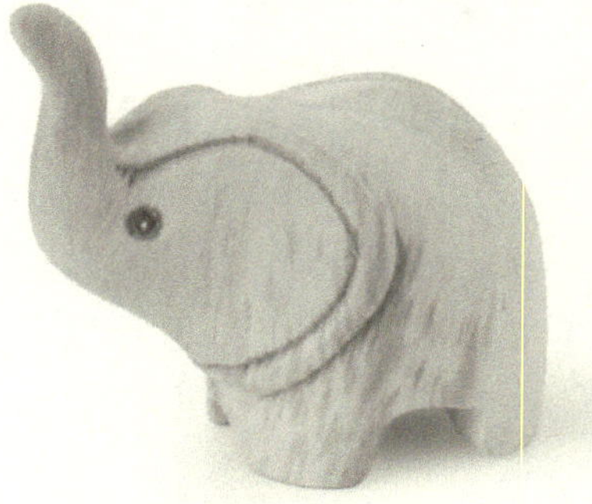

One of the big five animals, the elephant, is one of the most treasured animals globally and is considered the biggest mammal on land. Having this majestic animal in your home would be a perfect fit. The best part is that the procedure for making the elephant is not that difficult. Here is how you whittle an elephant.

The Required Materials

- Basswood
- Your whittling knife
- 10mm #7 gouge
- 10mm #6 gouge
- Wood safe mineral oil.

Procedure

1. Start by sketching the outline of the elephant on the piece of wood.
2. Use a band saw or a sharp whittling knife to carve out the front, back, top, and sides along the outline you've drawn.
3. Using the 10mm #7 gouge, shape the elephant according to the outline you've drawn.
4. Cut along the lines using a v tool to form the legs, ears, and tail.
5. Use a 10mm #6 gouge to rough out the major details and then add the head's major details.
6. Carve in the details of the hip and back areas until the carving looks like an elephant
7. Finally, add the wood-safe mineral oil.

Duck Carving

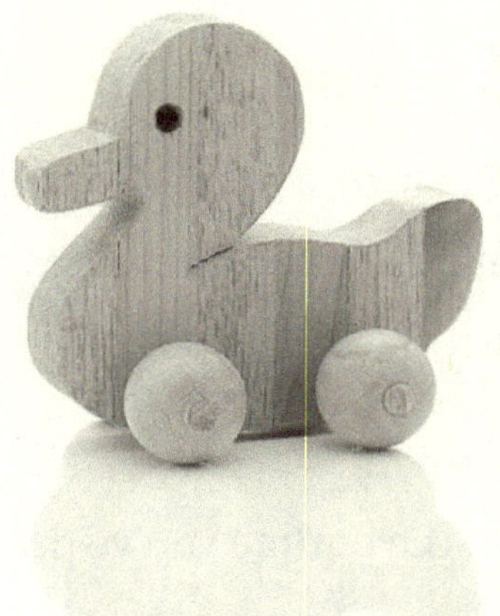

A duck is often regarded as one of the most colorful and beautiful birds. This species has many prominent features that make it a favorite among many collectors.

The Required Materials

- 71/2" by 4" by 13" cedar wood of choice
- 2" by 3" by 4" cedar wood
- Sand paper
- Carving knife
- Calipers
- V tool
- #3 or #5 gouge

Procedure

1. Start by sketching the image of the duck's head on the 2" by 3" by 4" cedar wood.
2. Carve in the details of the head using your whittling knife, then set the eyes in position and carve the mandible in place, then sand the whole head.
3. Sketch the duck's body on the piece of wood and carve out the primaries and the side pockets.
4. Continue shaping the primaries and side pockets before removing the lower edge of the primaries.
5. Now use wood glue to stick the head of the duck perfectly on the body.
6. Sand the whole carving and apply the safe wood finish.

A Majestic Buck

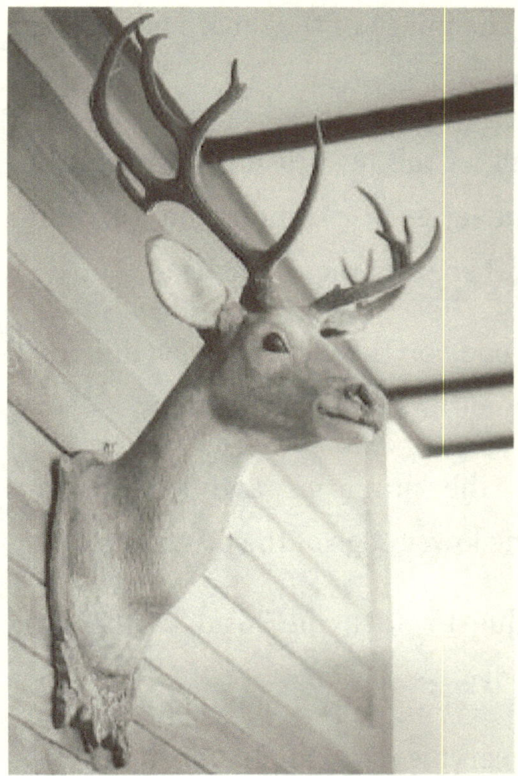

If you're a fan of wildlife, then this majestic hand carving project will definitely capture your fancy. The majestic nature of this animal gives it a unique touch that nobody can resist. It is a perfect project for anyone to try out because it is not only easy to carve but does not require a lot of work.

The Required Materials

- Basswood

- 10mm #7 gouge
- Whittling knife
- I/4" #7 gouge
- Wood safe mineral oil

Procedure

1. Trace the pattern of the deer onto the piece of basswood clearly marking the top, back, front and right side view.

2. Next, use the 10mm #7 gouge to rough out the deer's legs, neck, shoulders, hips, and knees.

3. Now carve the eyes sockets, nose, ears, and cheekbones using your whittling knife.

4. Continue to detail the eyes, mouth, and legs using your detailing knife.

5. Carefully carve the antlers on top of the deer's head, then burn in the rest of the facial expressions.

6. Sand the whole deer, then apply the wood-safe mineral oil.

A Dog

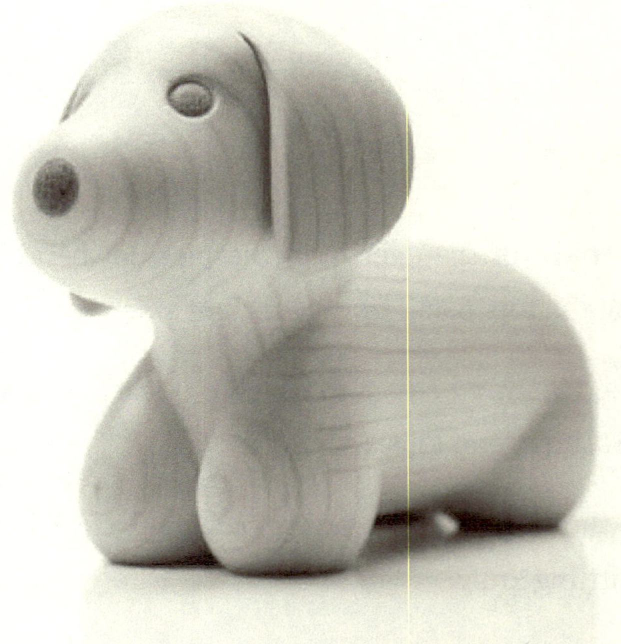

A dog is every man's best friend so having the carving of a dog is an excellent idea. Dogs have prominent features that give them a great touch. The best part is that it is straightforward to whittle a dog even for beginners.

The Required Materials

- Whittling knife
- Sandpaper

- Basswood
- Pencil
- Wood safe mineral oil

Procedure

1. Start by outlining the dog on the piece of wood.
2. Use your whittling knife to cut along the outline
3. Next, define the neck, legs, head, and tail by removing the excess wood using your detailing knife.
4. Make stop cuts along the face for the face and ears, then round and shape the head.
5. Rough out the body of the dog and legs by creating equal gouges between the legs. Rough out the tail as well.
6. Scoop out the eyes, then form the face and nose clearly.
7. Sand the whole carving using your sandpaper, then apply the wood finish oil.

Carving A Bunny

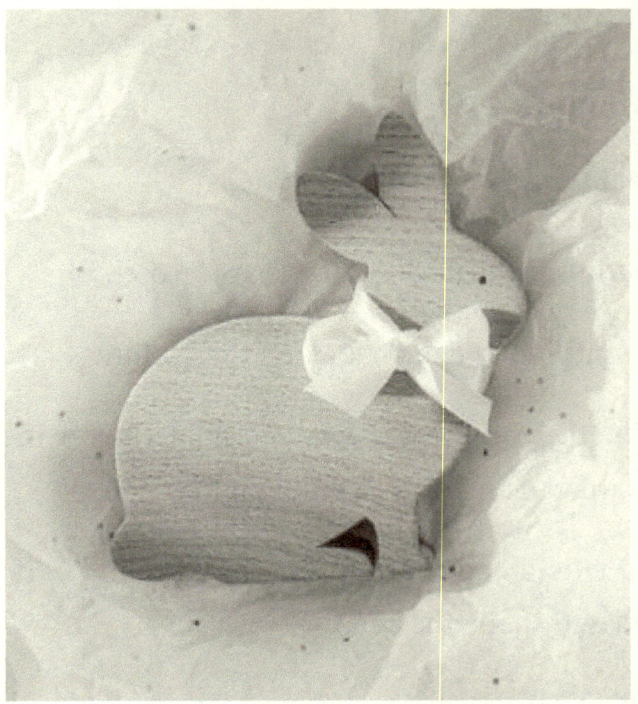

This is a fun project for a beginner whittler or expert looking to make several of them easily. The rabbit's body is symmetrical and straightforward thus does not require a lot of work or materials. You can make a small bunny to have as a souvenir or a big one to decorate your home.

The Required Materials

- Basswood
- Sandpaper

- Whittling knife
- Palm gouge
- Wood safe finish

Procedure

1. Transfer the bunny's pattern onto the piece of wood using the pencil while clearly marking all its features.
2. Use your whittling knife to carefully cut out the bunny outline while you remove the excess wood.
3. Make v cuts along the legs and remove the wood along the top and front of each leg before making them along with the head.
4. Continue making v cuts along with the corners of the front feet and chest.
5. Round the back to the centerline while working from top to bottom before making v cuts in front of the ears and around the head's top.
6. Rough out the entire bunny's body before rounding off the nose, front of the face, shoulder lines, backs of the ears, inside the ears, then finish in front of the head.

7. Continue detailing the bunny until it assumes the shape of the image above.

8. Once you're done, sand the whole bunny, then apply the wood-safe mineral oil.

Carving an Eagle

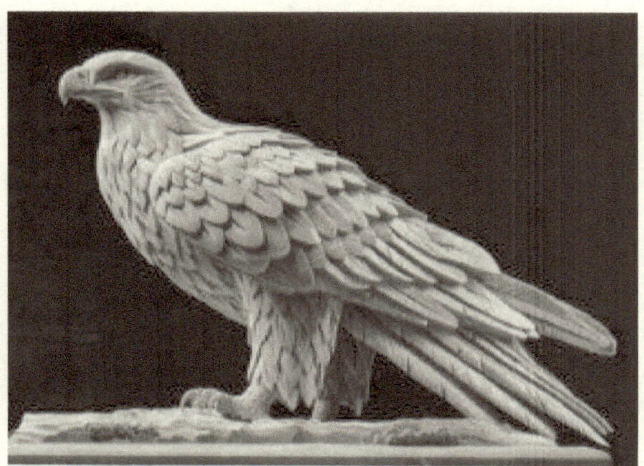

You'll definitely love carving an eagle because it is a classic symbol of freedom, and its nature makes it exciting and fun. Having its carving in your home or office would be great because of its great looks and the sense of power that it brings. The best part is that it is pretty easy to carve as long as you have the right wood.

The Required Materials

- A piece of hard maple or light hardwood of your choice
- Sand paper
- A whittling knife
- Pencil

- Wood safe finish

Procedure

1. Start by outlining the eagle on the piece of wood, clearly marking all its distinct features, just like in the picture above.
2. Now separate the wings using the bandsaw into two sections each before separating the feet as well.
3. Rough out and shape the wings by removing the excessive wood using your whittling knife.
4. Now move on to rough shape the head, tail, body, and feet using your detailing knife.
5. Slowly carve the talons; there are three talons in front and one at the back of each foot.
6. Next, carve the head and beak properly, then shape the eye sockets.
7. Define and burn in the wing and body feathers using your pencil before separating the feather tips.
8. Finally, sand the whole eagle, then apply the safe wood finish.

Carving a Whale

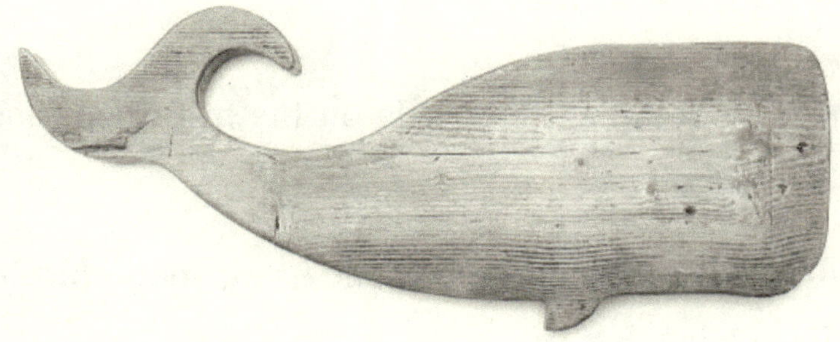

The whale is the largest mammal, and it inhabits more parts of the ocean than any other cetacean. Therefore, this animal's symbolic nature would be a perfect fit for your home or office. The best part is that carving the whale is very easy, although the carving of the body needs some attention to detail.

The Required Materials

- A basswood block for the body and fins
- Band saw
- Whittling knife
- Pencil
- Wood glue

- Acrylic paint
- Wood safe finish

Procedure

1. Begin by outlining the whale on the basswood block using your pencil.
2. Cut out the outline of the whale using your whittling knife or a bandsaw.
3. Rough out the body using your detailing knife until your project is smooth and shaped like a whale.
4. Now cut out the pectoral fins from the leftover basswood. Cut out the tail and dorsal fin as well from the basswood left.
5. Fix the pectoral, tail, and dorsal fins to the whale using wood glue in their appropriate position.
6. Now burn in the mouth, eyes, and gills on the whale using a drill bit or the sharp-pointed part of your knife.
7. Sand the whole whale using sandpaper, then apply the safe wood finish.

8. Use acrylic paint to paint the whale as you wish but most preferably black and white.

Carving a Goat

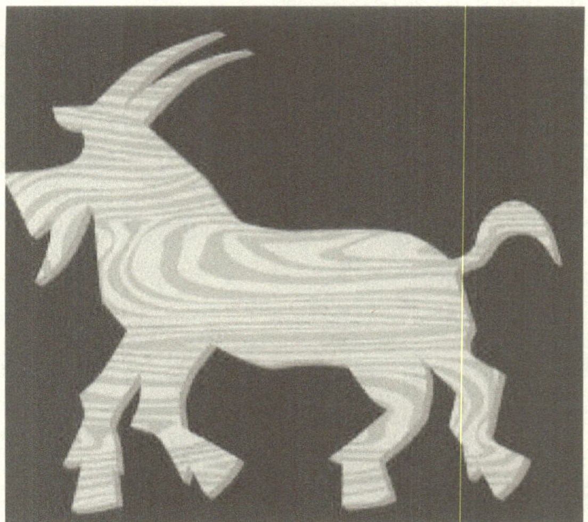

What makes carving a goat a great idea is this whimsical animal is full of personality. The best part is that the process of whittling a goat is so easy that a beginner can complete the project easily and even carve a whole herd in just a short while.

The Required Materials

- A block of basswood
- Wood glue
- Roughing out tools
- Whittling knife
- Sand paper

- Wood safe finish
- Acrylic paint

Procedure

1. Begin by making patterns of the goat onto the block, including the legs, ears, head, and horns.
2. Cut outside the outline using a band saw or whittling knife to remove the excess wood.
3. Rough out the goat's body by making rough cuts between the legs, where the legs meet the torso and around the tail.
4. Rough out the legs and create equal spaces between all the legs.
5. Round the neck and body using your whittling knife before shaping the back and tail.
6. Use your knife to shape the head, ears, neck, horns, and face. Make the horns slightly curved and use stop cuts to burn in the eyes, nose, and mouth.
7. Use sandpaper to smooth the entire goat, then apply the wood-safe finish.

8. Using acrylic paint, paint the goat as you like to enhance the appearance.

Wood Carving a Wolf

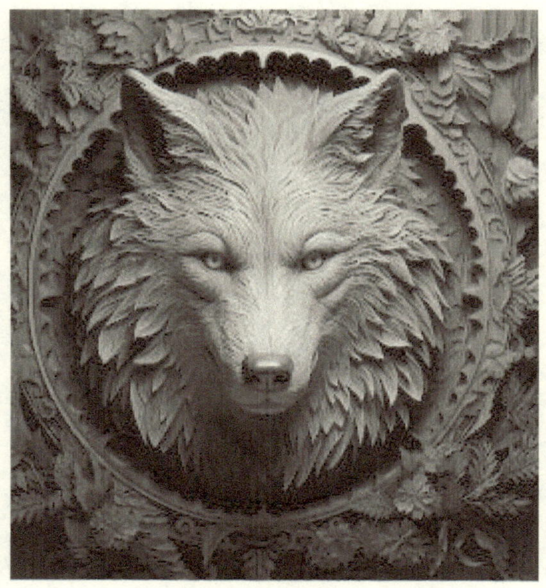

A wolf is a majestic animal that brings a certain unique sense of being stronger together. Having a wolf carving would definitely improve the appearance of a room. The best part is that it is easy to carve a wolf, and it is a great project in training on symmetry and proportions when it comes to whittling.

The Required Materials

- 2 by 5 by 8 basswood
- #9, #7, and #5 gouges
- Carving knife

- Acrylic paint

Procedure

1. Transfer the wolf pattern onto the basswood marking the head, tail, and legs.
2. Use a band saw or your whittling knife to cut along the lines you've drawn. Rough out the wolf by removing the excess wood and shaping the body.
3. Now shape the legs, upper part of the legs, tail, and rib cage. Make sure to shape the paws and legs as well using your detailing knife.
4. Shape the head, muzzle, and ears before carving the nose.
5. Carve in the mouth and refine the ears.
6. Add the basic fur texture and add the nose details.
7. Carve the toes on each foot, then carve the wolf's eyes.
8. Use acrylic paint to finish your carving.

American Bison

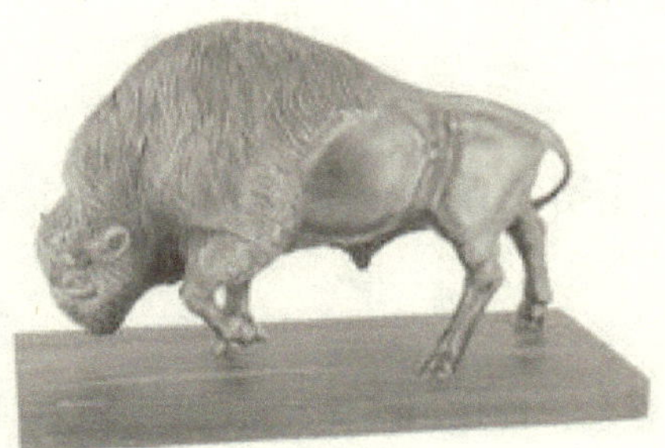

The bison, commonly mistaken for the buffalo, is a formidable beast and the heaviest land animal in North America. Its majestic posture gives it a sense of power and resilience that would make it a perfect carving to have. The structure and body of this animal make it fun and easy to carve.

The Required Materials

- A piece of bass wood
- Whittling knife
- Pencil
- Wood safe finish
- Sandpaper

Procedure

1. Start by outlining the bison on the piece of wood, clearly defining every part.
2. Cut out the outline of the top and side view by removing the excess wood.
3. Rough out the legs, tail, lower neck, and head using your whittling knife.
4. Shape the head, and the horns, then remove waste from the crosshatched areas.
5. Smooth out the major contours and features, then shape the four hooves into the same size and shape.
6. Burn in the nose and the horns of the bison before carving the eyes in place.
7. Sand the whole carving before applying the wood-safe finish.

Carving a Turtle

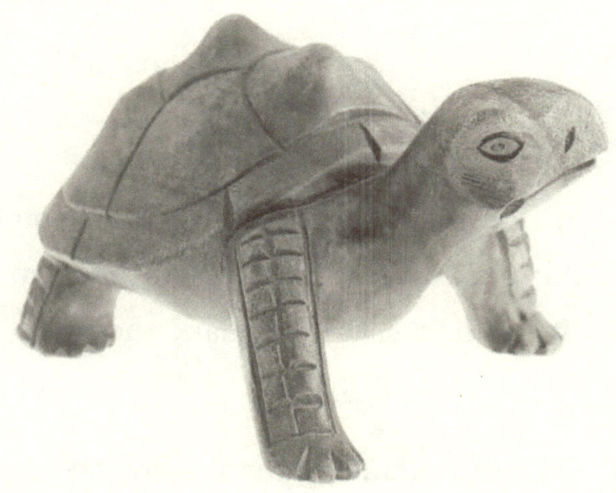

The turtle is a fascinating animal due to its slow nature and ability to withstand harsh climatic conditions for a long time. The turtle on a log is a good project idea for beginners because much of the carving is done using a whittling knife, and it incorporates all the carving cuts. You can also choose to whittle the turtle without the log but whittling the turtle on the block is much better.

The Required Materials

- 1 1/4" wide by 1 1/4" high by 3" block basswood
- Whittling knife
- V tool

- No 3 fish tail gouge
- Finishing materials (acrylic paint, liquid wax, and crylon)

Procedure

1. Start by drawing the pattern of the turtle on the piece of wood; make sure to lay the turtle at an angle to make it more lively, then mark the areas to carve away.
2. Use your carving knife to carve away the excess wood, and use the v tool to remove wood from the tight corners. Make sure to flatten the plane that represents the top of the log.
3. Continue removing as much wood as possible, making sure that the cuts are as perpendicular as possible.
4. Shape the top and underside of the head, then make a V-cut behind to define where it comes out of the shell. Round the shell as much as possible.
5. Start rounding the log, then make stop cuts to locate the tail and carve it to shape.
6. Carve around the shell to create the merging, then define the feet and legs.

7. Draw an octagon on top of the turtle's shell, then use the v-tool to define the lines drawn.

8. Burn in the mouth and eyes using a nail or the tip of your knife.

9. Apply the acrylic paint, preferably golden brown on the log and pale green on the shell.

Carving a Chickadee

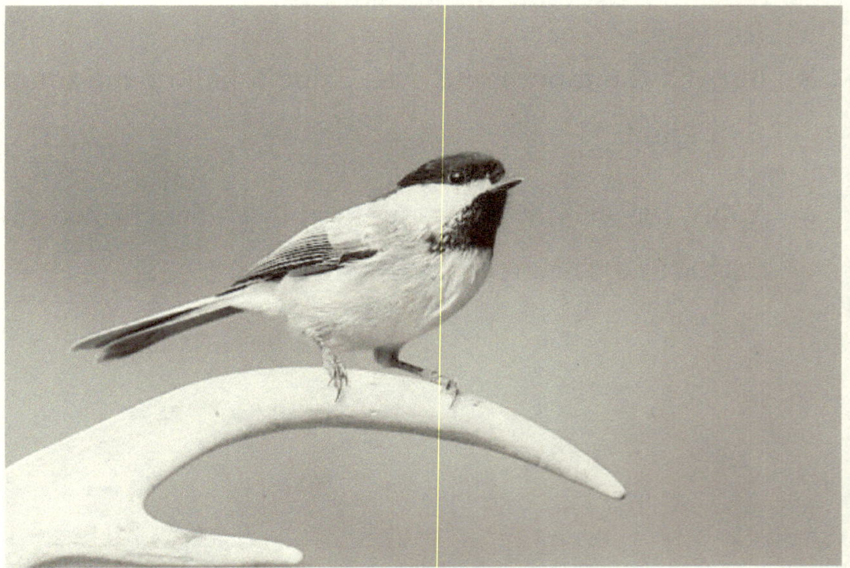

If you're a bird lover, then this project will definitely pick your liking. The bird is small and has a relatively simple color pattern that can brighten up any place. Carving it is so simple that even if you've never made a textured and straightforward bird before, you'll be able to make this attractive bird easily.

The Required Materials

- 2 ½" by 2 ½" by 3 ½" basswood
- Whittling knife
- Paints in assorted colors

- Band saw
- Bits

Procedure

1. Start by drawing the outline of the bird on the piece of wood, making sure that you line up the ends of each view.
2. Drill a hole within the circular area through the side view.
3. Cut out the bird's outline using a band saw or your whittling knife, then draw a line around the carving block.
4. Draw the extremes of all the areas that will be relieved away, such as the wings, head, and tail top. After which, relieve all those areas, including the tail and feet.
5. Rough out all the carving areas, then round the body properly, then smooth all the parts using a sanding material.
6. Draw feather groups across the entire bird in proportion, then relieve the feathers away from the body.

7. Use the bit to shape the eye mounds and eyelid line, then texture the feathers starting from the rear to the forward.

8. Finally, apply the paints on the bird as you see fit.

Carving a Pig

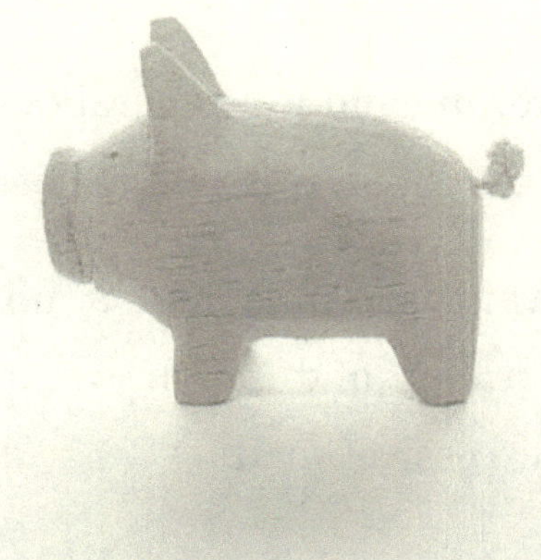

Whittling a pig is a great idea, especially for a beginner, as it doesn't have a difficult general layout, and you only need a whittling knife. If you love pork or you are a pig keeper, then this project is for you. You can either decide to put hair or paint on the pig, but you can also leave it all-natural without anything.

The Required Materials

- Whittling knife
- 2 1/4" by 3 ¼" by 5 ½" basswood
- No 7 and 9 gouge
- Band saw

- Sandpaper
- Wood safe finish

Procedure

1. Draw the centerline and the general outline of the pig, including the snout, feet, and the ears front.
2. Using your whittling knife and a no. 7 gouge, proceed to cut out and rough out the pig by removing the excessive wood.
3. Redraw the centerline before locating the major features.
4. Use the v tool, knife, and no. 7 gouge to outline the ridge, tail, and feet, then detail them correctly.
5. Shape the end of the snout and shape the head and burn in the mouth and nostrils.
6. Carve the remainder of the head and shape the eyes in place.
7. Carve the wood in the legs to separate them from the body and each other and use the v tool to separate and outline the hooves.

8. Round the body and carve the tail in place while using the v tool to outline it.

9. Finally, sand the whole carving, then apply the wood-safe finish.

Carving a snail

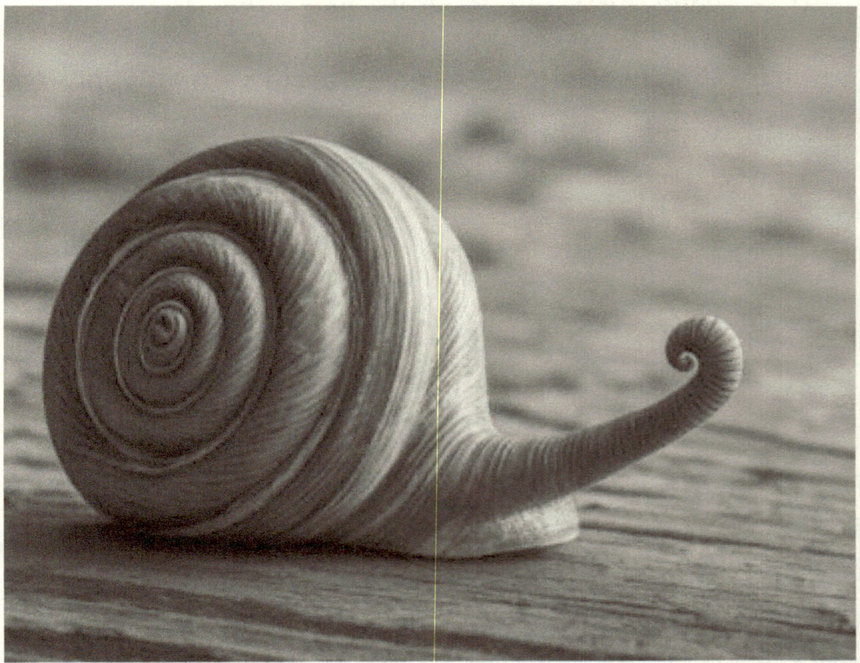

Not so many people love the snail because of its slime. However, it has a shell that is attractive, which most people love. Also, carving a snail is relatively easy and is suitable for practicing whittling cuts.

The Required Materials

- Carving knife
- Band saw
- Carving gouge

- Piece of wood
- Abrasives
- Wood safe finish

Procedure

1. Transfer the outline of the snail onto the piece of wood, then use the bandsaw or your whittling knife to cut out the outline.
2. Rough out the entire carving to remove the excess wood, including the shell and the head.
3. Continue shaping the shell, then draw the spiral pattern you need before using a v tool to carve out the spiral areas.
4. After shaping the shell as much as you can, move on to shape the back then the head.
5. Mount the tentacles in place, then continue carving away the wood you don't need around the snail's head and its body.
6. Continue roughing out the body, then move on to the backside.

7. Finally, sand the whole carving and apply the wood-safe finish.

Whittling a Bass Fish

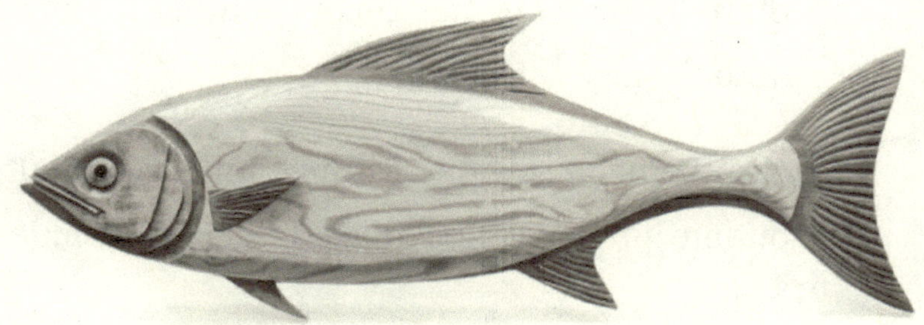

If you are a big fan of aquatic animals, then you will definitely like this project. Not only is it a great decorative piece but also a great whittling idea for beginners. This is because it is effortless to whittle a fish, and the carving process does not require a lot of materials.

The Required Materials

- A carving knife
- Basswood
- Gouges of various sizes
- V tool
- Band saw
- Wood safe finish

Procedure

1. Start by drawing the general outline of the fish onto the piece of wood.
2. Use the band saw or whittling knife to cut out the outline properly, and don't forget to include the head.
3. Redraw the outline again while giving priority to the head and its key points.
4. Rough out the entire carving using your whittling knife, then begin defining the certain areas of the head that include the mouth, eyes, and gills.
5. Continue detailing the head and other parts of the fish before carving the remaining fins from the leftover wood.
6. Attach the fins to the fish using wood glue, then use your carving knife to burn in the veins and other features.
7. Sand the entire carving and apply the wood-safe finish.

Whittling a Shark

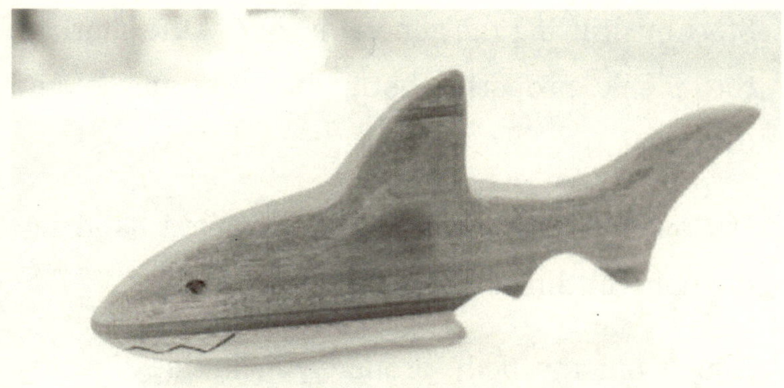

This fascinating animal is one of the most dangerous animals in the sea due to its predatory nature. However, it is also a symbol of strength and power, and therefore it would make the perfect decorative piece for any home or office. The process of carving a shark is so simple that any beginner can do it, and it is also great for practicing your whittling skills.

The Required Materials

- A whittling knife
- Basswood or any other wood
- Sandpaper
- A pencil
- V tool

Procedure

1. Start by drawing the general layout of the shark on the blank properly, both the side views and overview.

2. Cut out the outline of the shark using a band saw or your whittling knife.

3. Rough out the body properly, including the fins, which should be pointed, and the head too.

4. Continue roughing out the body, then burn in the mouth using the v tool before defining the tail properly.

5. Carve in the gills and other key aspects of the head, including the eyes.

6. Sand the whole carving, then apply the wood-safe finish.

Whittling a Small Dinosaur

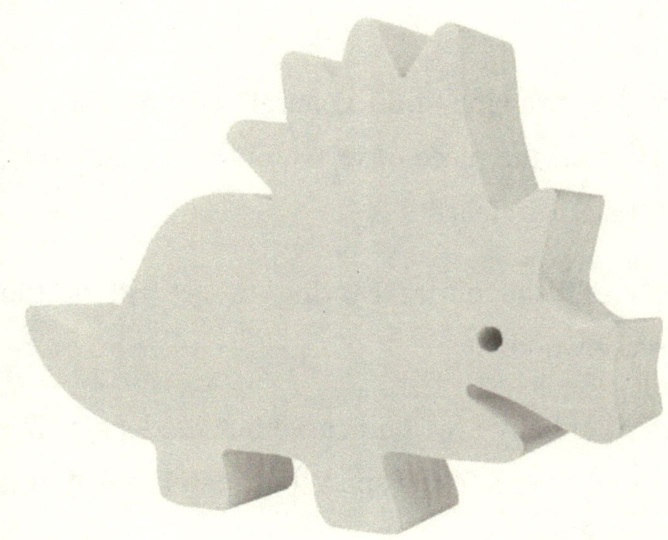

The dinosaur is believed to have existed centuries ago before they became extinct. They are thought to be huge majestic animals that roamed the lands. Therefore, to have a carving of this dinosaur is to have a piece of our history as humans. Plus, it is an amazing decorative object.

The Required Materials

- Basswood
- Whittling knife
- Sandpaper
- V tool

- Wood safe finish

Procedure

1. Start by drawing the general outline of the dinosaur on the piece of wood, outlining the arms, head, and legs clearly.
2. Rough out the entire carving to get rid of the excessive wood.
3. Round the belly area and carve out the legs, using the v tool to create the space between the feet and clearly defining them.
4. Carve out the small arms, thin out the neck area, and continue carving and roughing out the head.
5. Burn in the eyes and the mouth using your whittling knife.
6. Continue to rough out the entire carving until you get rid of the excess wood.

Whittling a Cat

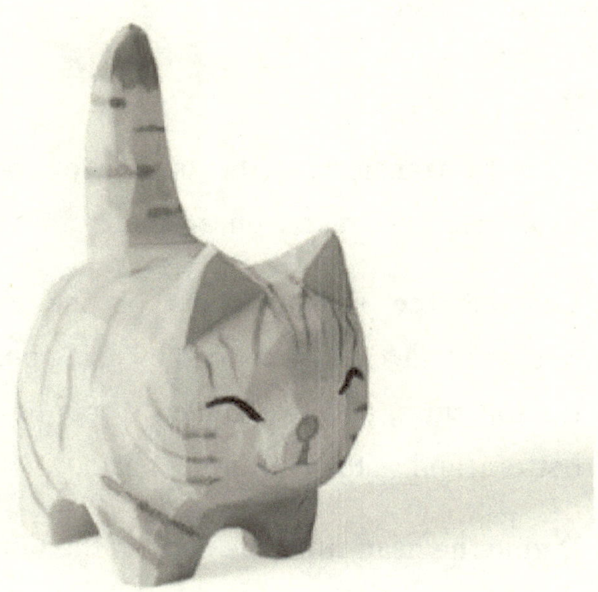

We are all familiar with cats; they are amazing animals to have around in your home. And if you are a cat lover, then this project will definitely be perfect for you.

The Required Materials

- A whittling knife
- A selection of gouges
- Sandpaper

- Basswood
- V tool
- Wood safe finish

Procedure

1. Start by transferring the outline of the cat and make reference marks on the piece of wood.
2. Cut out the rough details of the carving by removing the excessive wood by using push cuts on the top sides, and two angled v cuts to define the bottom, and a stop cut for the head.
3. Define the head from the back of the block around the chin and the ears.
4. Round the front of the body by removing the excess wood from the front and back of the head.
5. Carve in the tail and legs in front of the cat, then use the v tool to separate the legs from the body.
6. Continue detailing the cat, then burn in the eyes and mouth before carving the inside and back areas of the ears.

7. Carve the nose and add the other key features of the face and head in general.

8. Sand the whole carving, then apply the wood-safe finish.

Carving a Mouse

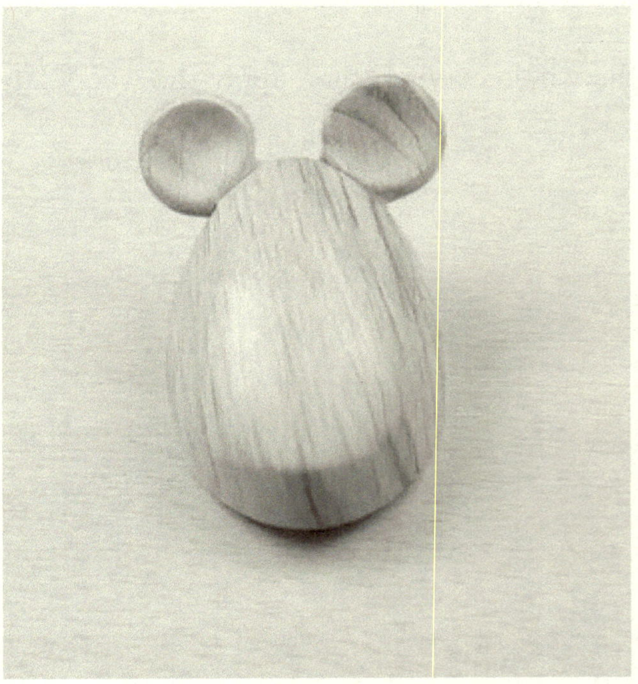

Not many people love mice, and that is understandable because they can be very pesky and destructive. However, looking at them from a different perspective, they usually do look kind of cute. Therefore, it wouldn't be such a bad idea for you to sculpt a mouse not only because it would make for a great decorative piece, but you'll also get to practice your whittling skills.

The Required Materials

- Whittling knife

- A block of wood
- Wood safe finish
- V tool
- A selection of gouges

Procedure

1. Start by drawing the rough outline of the mouse on all sides of the block of wood.
2. Using a band saw or a sharp whittling knife, carve out the profile following the outline you had drawn.
3. Now continue rounding the body and head of the mouse using your whittling knife.
4. Burn in the ears using your gouge and your whittling knife until they are erect and well rounded.
5. Using your v tool, make stop cuts along where the legs should start, separating the legs and the body and then carving in the legs.

6. Behind the mouse, carve in the small tail of the mouse using your gouge to separate it from the body and your whittling knife to carve it out.
7. Now burn in the key features of the face, including the eyes, nose, and mouth.
8. Finally, sand the whole carving and apply a wood-safe finish.

Carving a Dolphin

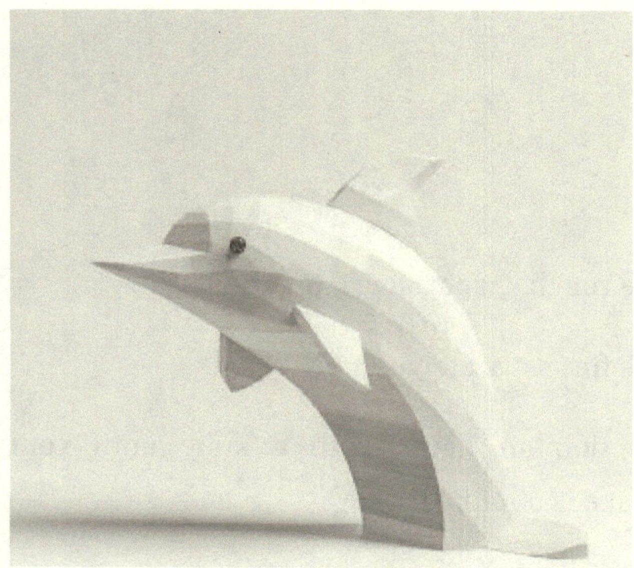

This one is for any dolphin enthusiasts out there. It could be you are a dolphin lover and are looking to incorporate that into your life. If so, this is your project. This beautiful sculpture is suitable for home decor or office decoration, or you can also gift it to your dolphin lover friends. This is a bottle-nosed dolphin, and it passes as one of the biggest and most common dolphins. It is found in shallow coastal waters and deep oceans.

The Required Materials

- Driftwood
- Band saw

- Knife
- Sandpaper
- Dowels

Procedure

1. Cut out the rough shape using a band saw.
2. Cut out the fins separately.
3. Carve the dolphin figure with a knife until your desired shape is obtained.
4. After carving, sand the figure.
5. Attach the fins.
6. Clean and sand the local driftwood on which the dolphin will be attached.
7. You can cut the driftwood into the shape of your choice.
8. Mount the carved dolphin on the driftwood using the dowels.

Carving a Horse/Unicorn

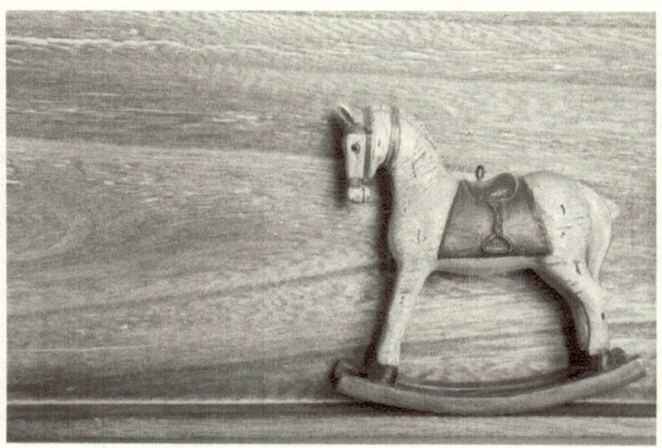

A unicorn is such a prestigious sculpture, and you might want to give this one a try. Although it is a mythical creature, it has been attributed to a symbol of purity and grace, fantasy, or rarity. That is why diving into this project is as unique and glamorous as it sounds. This one is also for the horse lovers out there. It can serve as the perfect office decoration. Who wouldn't love this piece as a gift?

The Required Materials

- Whittling knife
- Sandpaper for that smooth finish
- Band Saw
- Pencil

- Glue

Procedure

1. Trace a figure of the unicorn on a piece of wood.
2. Cut it out with a band saw as you follow the direction of the grain.
3. Using your pencil, draw the block in the center and begin to carve the head with the whittling knife of your choice.
4. Make sure to carve out the unicorn's horn and leave room for the mane if you so wish to.
5. Carve the belly and the back.
6. Using your band saw, cut the opening between the legs and carve with a knife.
7. Cut the tail separately and only attach it when you are done carving the full body.
8. You can use glue to stick it in.

Whittling a Pelican

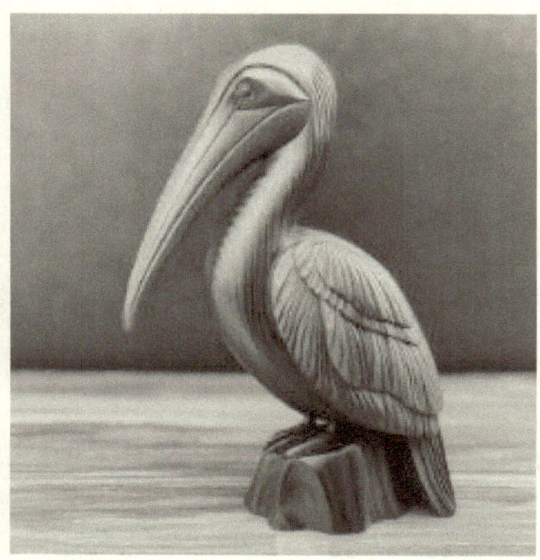

Did you know that pelicans use their pouch to catch food tossed by humans? I'm sure this is your first time hearing that. Adding to the fact that pelicans are brilliant birds, this is a perfect opportunity to immerse yourself in the bird world. This sculpture could serve as an excellent home decoration piece since not many would whittle a pelican because of its oddly looking shape. This project might just be what you need to unlock your expert whittling skills. Dive in!

The Required Materials

A block of wood

Whittling knife

Band saw

Sandpaper

Paint to spice up your sculpture

Varnish

Procedure

1. Cut the pattern from the block of wood following the direction of the grain.
2. Block out and form the wings. Attach the tops slightly.
3. Carve the bill and the pouch before working on the neck and head.
4. Make sure to give the bill about ¾ inch through the middle section.
5. To form the mouth, extend V-shaped cuts extending almost to the eyes.
6. Cut the feet roughly to give the bird stability and provide a base for the sculpture.
7. Give the bird some web toes.
8. Using your sandpaper, smooth out your sculpture except on the wings.

9. The wings should be rough and clear knife-cuts visible.

10. To add spice to your sculpture, paint the pouch and feet orange in color, and the tail and wings tips black to give it that authentic finish.

11. Varnish your sculpture, and it's good to go.

Whittling a Mama and a Baby Kangaroo

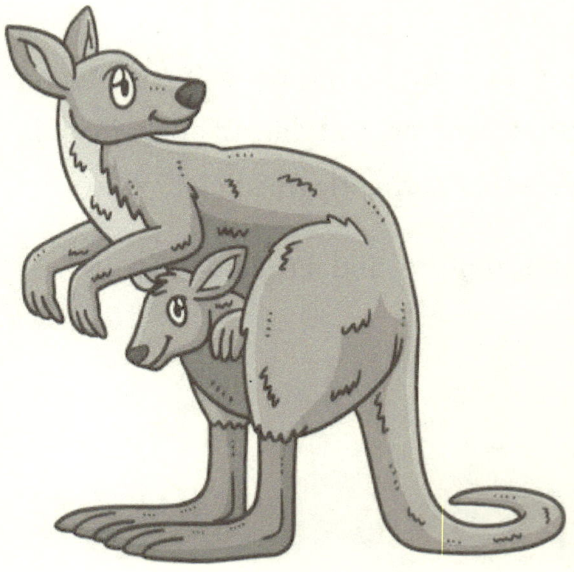

Did you know that a baby kangaroo is also known as a joey? Did you also know that only the female kangaroos have pouches and not the male ones? These are some interesting facts about the kangaroos that I thought you should know. You can dive deep into this project as you explore more about kangaroos. This project is for those who specifically want to try something out of the ordinary and would like to put their whittling abilities to the test.

The Required Materials

- Whittling knife
- Piece of softwood

- Sandpaper
- Band saw

Procedure

1. Place the pattern on the wood and carve out the shape.
2. Carve the head and the ears.
3. Begin carving the pouch with the baby kangaroo inside it.
4. Ensure the tail and hind legs are big enough to support the weight of the sculpture so that it can stand freely.
5. Carve the forelimbs such that they are small and fall just above the joey's head.
6. Round out your sculpture to give it a smooth finish.

Carving Little People

Carving a Gnome

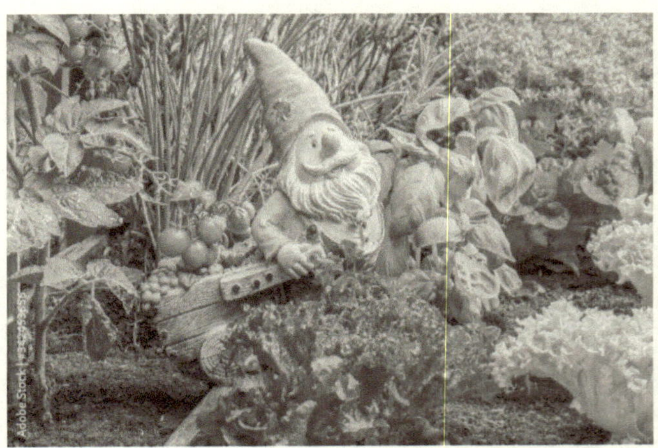

Many European cultures have their folklore that usually includes little people. The Irish have the *leprechaun*, the Norwegian have the *nisse,* and the Swedes have the *tomte.* In Scandinavian countries, these gnomes, for the most part, were friendly, unlike the trolls. They used to help around the farms, but if they got mistreated, they became mischievous. Carving them would be a great idea since they are easy to carve, and you also get to practice your whittling skills.

The Required Materials

- A carving knife
- Basswood block of about 2 ½" by 3" by 6 ½"

- Micro v tool
- A selection of gouges
- Acrylic paints

Procedure

1. Start by outlining the gnome on the block, including the front, back, and side views.
2. Cut out the profile of the gnome using a band saw to remove the excess wood.
3. Redraw the outline of the gnome while highlighting the key features, including the beard, face, hands, and feet.
4. Begin to rough out the feet, then block in the shoes before blocking in the ears.
5. Start working on the hat by rounding it to form a cone, then making cuts on both sides of the centerline to give the face its angle.
6. Block in the arms, then separate them from the body using the v tool, repeat the same when separating the fingers.

7. Round the hem of the coat, then burn in the nose and the eyes.

8. Relieve the mustache from the beard and carve in the mouth before outlining the eyebrows and hair strands.

9. Continue roughing out the beard, mustache, sideburns, and face.

10. Finally, apply the wood-safe finish.

Carving a Viking

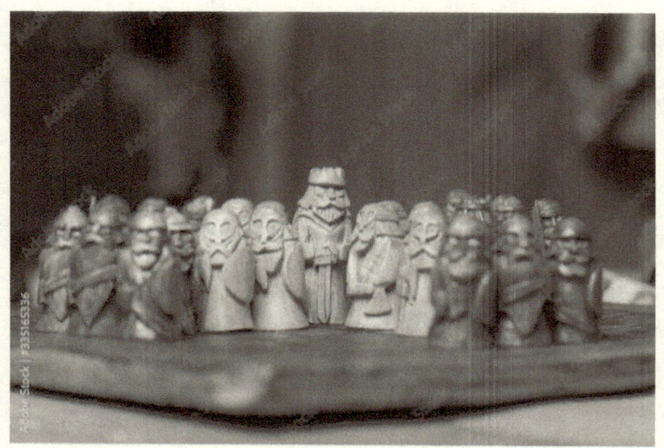

There are many approaches when it comes to carving a Viking, but the best is the warrior. They are known for their great strength in battle and are considered to have existed a century ago. Therefore, a carving of a Viking would be great for a decorative piece. In addition, the process of sculpting a Viking is easy.

The Required Materials

- Basswood block of about 3" by 4" by 9"
- Carving knife
- V tool
- Acrylic paint
- #5 gouge

Procedure

1. Draw the general outline of the Viking on the piece of wood, then use the band saw to cut out the two profiles.
2. Draw the centerline on the front and back, then locate the main features such as the beards and arms.
3. Rough out the carving to remove the excess wood before carving in the arms and the hands. Use the v tool to separate the arms from the body.
4. Carve out the feet and the legs while defining the features using the v tool.
5. Now move to the face to define the cheeks by carving the angles that carry the cheeks at 90°.
6. Define the eye mounds by cutting away wood on the sides of the nose, then relieve the mustache from the beard.
7. Carve in the eyes, then outline them with a detail knife.
8. Continue to detail the beard with a small v tool, then carve the leggings bindings with the v tool.
9. Apply the wood-safe finish.

Stackable Santa

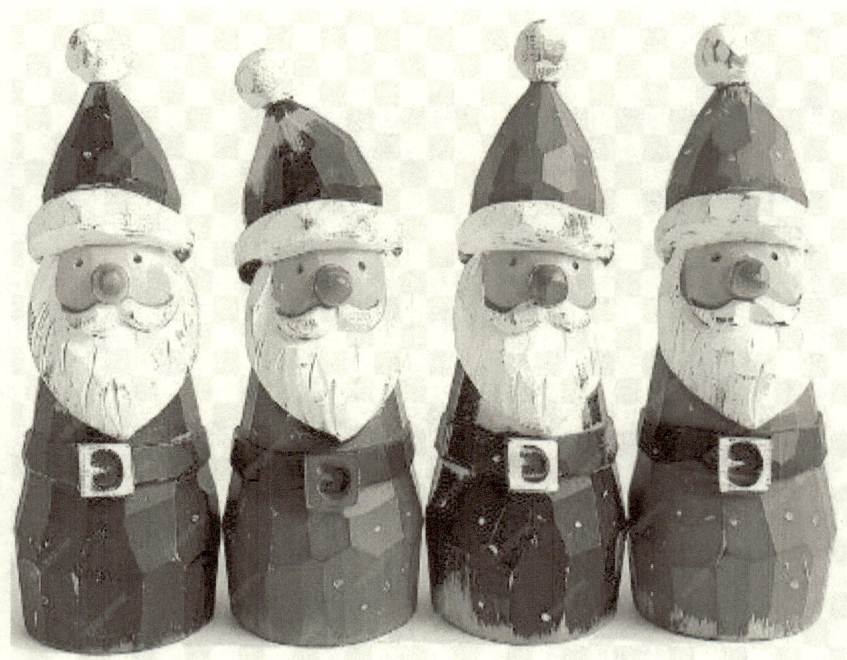

During the Christmas holidays, people normally decorate their homes and workplaces to commemorate the festivities. However, it can be a real hustle or quite expensive to keep purchasing them. Therefore, the next best thing is to make your own decorations that are customized to your liking. This project is easy to make and does not require a lot of materials.

The Required Materials

- Whittling knife
- No 5 3mm gouge and no 9 5mm gouge
- Basswood
- V tool
- Wood safe finish
- Acrylic paint

Procedure

1. Start by drawing the general outline of Santa on the piece of wood.
2. Use a band saw or a sharp whittling knife to cut out the general outline, including brim, head belt, and boots.
3. Draw a centerline so that it divides Santa's body into two equal parts.
4. Carve the hair on the sides and back of the head, then mark the outer edges of the forehead and mustache.

5. Use the v tool to define the mustache clearly, then continue rounding the eyebrows and cheeks above the mustache.

6. Round the corners of the cap, then reestablish the arms using the v tool.

7. Continue to round the shoulders and the chest area, then go ahead and carve the mittens.

8. Round the stomach region as well, then carve the edges of the buckle as well.

9. Carve in the boots, make sure to notch the heels, and angle the soles up bottom towards the toes.

10. Outline the tops of Santa's soles and heels, then shape the boot toes.

11. Add the details to the general carving, such as dimples, brim, and cuffs.

12. Finally, paint the carving using acrylic paint.

Fireman Carving

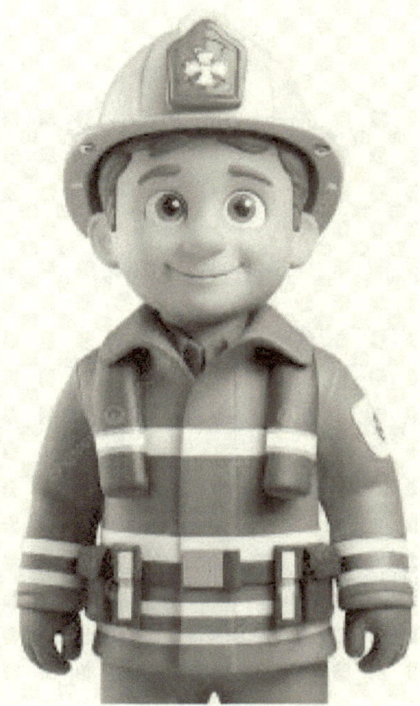

Many unsung heroes deserve our appreciation and gratitude because many lives would be lost or destroyed without them. Some of these include firefighters who risk their lives to save those of others from fire.

Therefore, having the carving of a fireman would be a great way of appreciating them, but still, it makes for a great decoration piece. It is easy to whittle and allows you to practice all the whittling cuts.

The Required Materials

- Basswood
- Band saw
- Whittling knife
- A selection of gouges
- Wood safe finish
- Acrylic paint

Procedure

1. Begin by outlining the fireman on the piece of wood, then use the band saw to remove the extra wood.
2. Use a v tool to remove the extra wood around the hat to create the brim, then round them off.
3. Start detailing the neck, ears, and mustache, then establish the eyes by creating the eye mounds.
4. Continue detailing the nose, then the ears, thin down the brim to expose the ears, and separate the sideburns from the ears.

5. Trim the mustache to reveal the mouth, then define the lower lip before removing more wood from the eyebrows.

6. Once you are done with the key features of the head, carve in the collar to give it shape

7. Continue detailing the whole carving until every feature is clearly distinct.

8. Finish by applying the wood-safe finish and paint as you like.

Carving Saint Nicholas

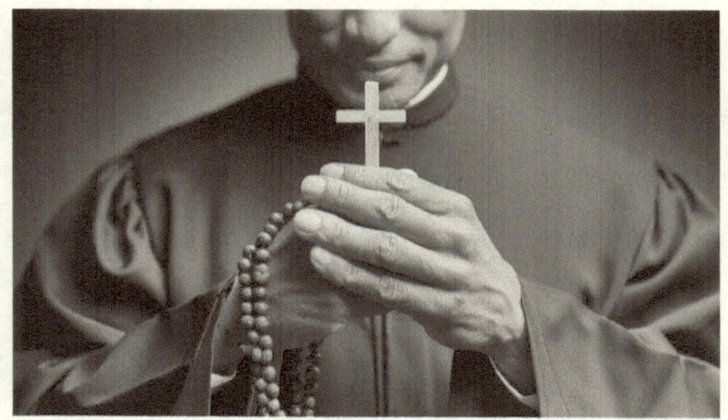

If you're a strong Catholic believer, then this project is perfect for you. If you need something to use while praying or making your home more Christian-like, then this carving is for you.

However, if you don't have a solid Christian faith, it would also make for a great decorative piece. Moreover, it is quite easy to sculpt for any beginner and practice the various whittling cuts.

The Required Materials

- Basswood
- A selection of gouges
- Band saw
- Whittling knife

- Wood safe finish

Procedure

1. Start by drawing the general outline on the piece of wood to act as a guide for the whittling procedure. Use a band saw to cut out the extra unnecessary wood.

2. The next step is to burn in the important parts, including the hat, coat, hands, and feet.

3. Carve in the hands and use the v tool to separate it from the body. The left hand will hold a pole; so, form a fist and drill a hole in the middle.

4. Now burn in the face and its key features; this includes the eyes, mouth, and nose. Make sure to carve in the sideburns to separate the beard from the ears.

5. Carve in the ears and shape the beard to the right size. Make sure to detail the hat properly according to the picture as well as the beard.

6. Smooth out the middle part of the carving, then carve in the coat and the belt properly. After which, carve the feet as well below the coat.

7. Fine-tune the whole carving using your whittling knife to make sure you don't miss out on the key features.

8. Finally, apply the wood-safe finish.

Carving Roscoe

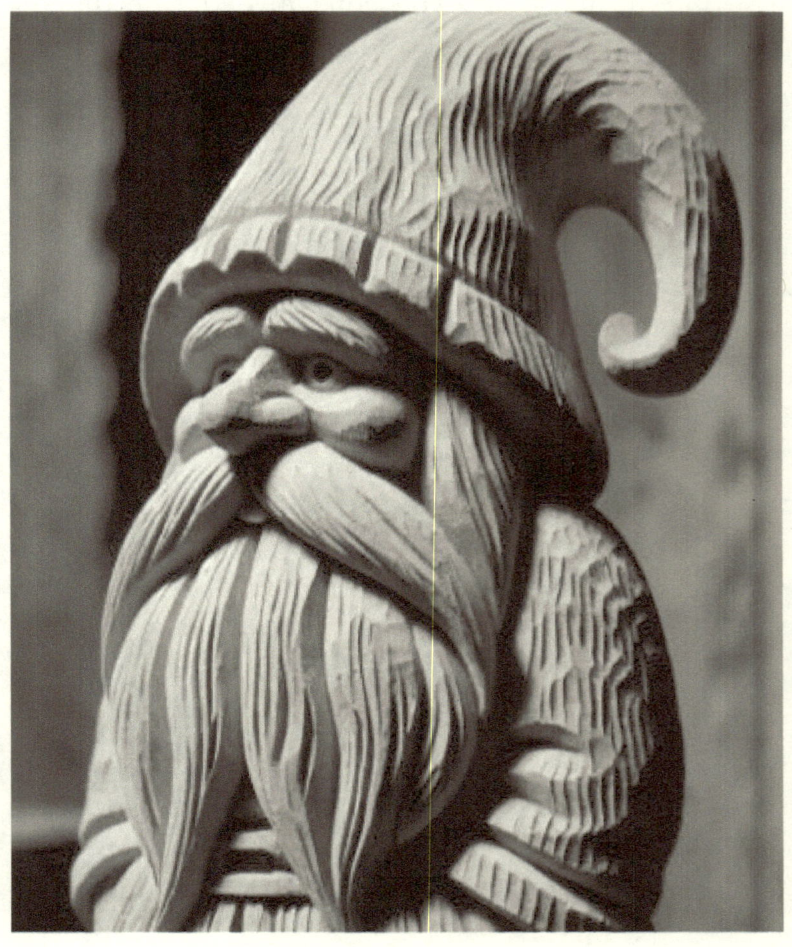

If you're into humorous or weird characters, then you'll definitely love this roscoe carving. He's a character in most movies that is usually sloppy, slow, or humorous. Therefore, he'll make a good decoration piece for your home or office. Moreover, the carving process is easy for any beginner.

The Required Materials

- Basswood
- Whittling knife
- V tool
- Acrylic paint
- A selection of gouges

Procedure

1. Begin by drawing the general outline of roscoe on the piece of wood, then use a band saw or your whittling knife to remove the excess wood.
2. Use the v tool to cut the base and separate the legs and also the hat brim.
3. Establish the arms, then separate the shoes before roughing the face.
4. Clean up the brim around the face and nose, then do the same to the front and back.
5. Separate the legs, both front and back, then shape the hat to the finished size.

6. Make the cuffs by cutting around each pair of pants, then make cuts straight into the face on each side of the nose.

7. Finish the nose, then around the mouth area before shaping the chin.

8. Carve in the clothes both back, and front then cut some patches.

9. Continue detailing the main features and sand the whole carving.

10. Apply the wood-safe finish.

Carving a Caricature Football Player

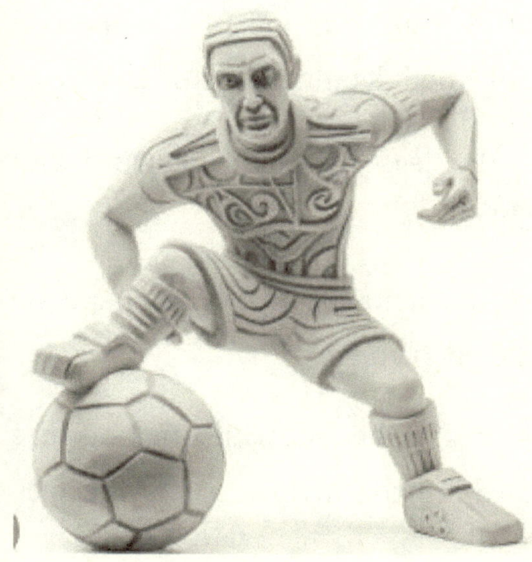

Are you into sports? If so, this football player caricature would be a fantastic piece to have as a souvenir or a decorative piece. Whichever design you choose to make is up to you, but this is the design you're going to whittle in this book.

The Required Materials

- 3" by 12" long basswood
- Whittling knife
- V tool
- A selection of gouges

Procedure

1. Start by drawing the rough outline of the football player on the piece of wood detailing the key features.
2. Round and shape the legs using the sharper and longer side of your blade.
3. Rough in the edges using a no 11 gouge, then shape the face as well using the no. 9 gouge.
4. Burn in the key features of the face while making sure to properly define where the helmet meets the face with your knife.
5. Using stop cuts, draw the chin and jaw lines, then shape it to the shirt.
6. Shape and detail the helmet using your knife.
7. Burn in the fingers and the ball using a v tool and the no. 11 gouge.
8. Now move to detail the shirt and the pants using your v tool and stop cuts with your knife.
9. Shape the shoes, use your knife, and then use your v tool to detail the entire carving correctly.
10. Finally, apply the wood-safe finish.

Carving an Elf

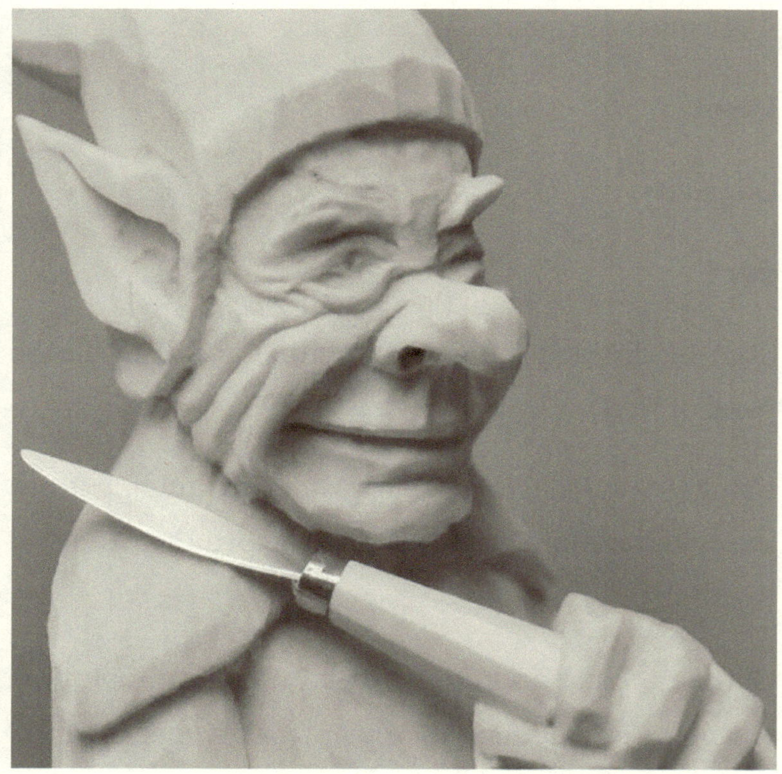

Aside from Santa, the elf is also an essential part when it comes to Christmas holidays. Therefore, carving an elf in addition to Santa would make for an excellent decorative piece. Moreover, whittling an elf is also relatively easy and does not require a lot of materials.

The Required Materials

- Basswood or any other softwood

- Whittling knife
- A selection of gouges
- V tool
- Oil paint

Procedure

1. Start by drawing the general outline of the elf on the piece of wood.
2. Using a band saw or a sharp whittling knife, cut out the rough outline of the elf and remove the excessive wood.
3. Outline the hat and the forehead using a v tool, then create the eye mounds and the top of the cheeks.
4. Burn in the key features of the face, including the mouth and the eyes
5. Outline the beard using the no 15 gouge, then use a no 12 gouge to rough out the fringe of the hat.
6. Use a no 8 to recess the area of the left arm, then shape the bent legs.
7. Establish the boots, then shape them properly using your knife.

8. Separate the legs evenly and do the undercutting on the jackets with the no 15 v tool.

9. Continue detailing the features of the elf clearly, then separate the fingers as well.

10. Apply the wood-safe finish.

Carving a Wizard

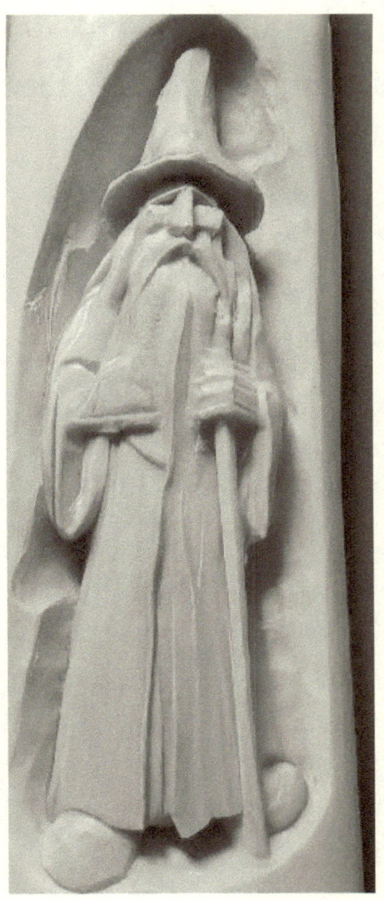

If you're a fan of mystic arts, then you'll love this project. The wizard is an amazing decorative piece to have around, or you can make a small one to have as a key holder. Additionally, the project is perfect for teaching basic skills in carving and is ideal for demonstration purposes.

The Required Materials

- Whittling knife of your choice
- ¾" by ¾" by 24" basswood
- Pencil.
- Small v tool
- Strop

Procedure

1. Start by drawing the rough outline of the wizard on the piece of wood, then use a band saw to cut through the outline and get rid of the excess wood.
2. Outline the bottom of the hat by making deep stop cuts 2 ½" from the segment's bottom.
3. Now relieve the face up to the hat, then cut to the stop cuts to create space for the eye sockets and cheeks.
4. Shape the face by cutting up to the stop cut to remove about 3/16" from both sides of the face.
5. Define the bottom of the nose by making a deep stop cut on the front corner down to the bottom of the hat.
6. Next, outline the eyes and nose by starting at the inside corner of the eye and make stop cuts for each eye.

7. Move to shape the cheeks and the nose using the tip of your knife, then remove a chip from each side of the nose so that where the cuts intersect will be the eye socket.

8. Outline the mustache, then cut down to the stop cut to separate the mustache and the cheeks.

9. Shape the beard by cutting up to the stop cuts under the mustache, using your small v tool or the tip of your knife. Add texture and hairlines to the beard and mustache.

10. Finally, shape the nose by shaving the top to create the nose's bridge and detail the hat by carving it to a point. Make sure to make the hat squashed down, folded, and evenly folded at the top.

Other Whittling Projects

Carving an apple

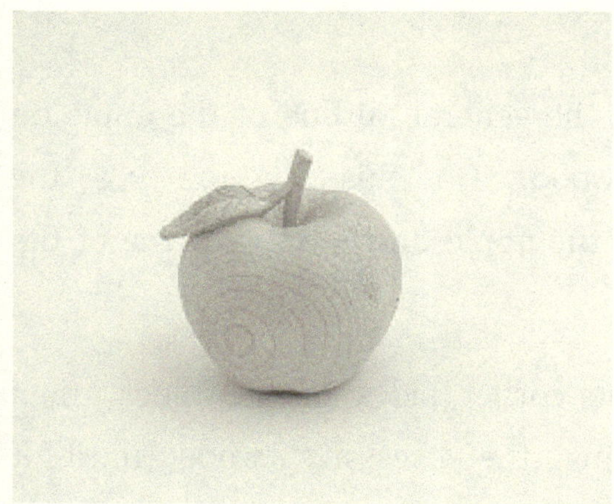

If you're looking for a great decorative piece that will add a nice touch to your kitchen, then carving an apple is perfect. If you can have this apple together with other fruits on your countertop, it will greatly improve the ambiance of your home.

The Required Materials

- A block of wood (50 by 50 by 300)
- Whittling knife
- V tool
- A selection of gouges

- Wood safe finish
- Sandpaper

Procedure

1. Start by drawing the general outline of the apple on the piece of wood. Do this by drawing the circumference of the apple on the top surface of the block.

2. Now, remove the corner sides of the block, then continue removing the excessive wood until it becomes cylindrical.

3. Using the v gouge, start rounding off the block from one sideline to the adjacent corner line.

4. Refine the cylinder using the no.3 gouge before using your whittling knife and the v tool to burn in the leaves.

5. Below the leaves, draw a line around the cylinder to estimate the width. Turn to the lower half and draw a line around the cylinder for the lower half of the apple.

6. Next, chop in from either side of the line using a no. 3 gouge until it is smooth and well rounded.

7. Continue to refine the general shape of the apple until it is well rounded.

8. Sand the whole carving, then apply the wood-safe finish.

Forest Spirit Wood Carving

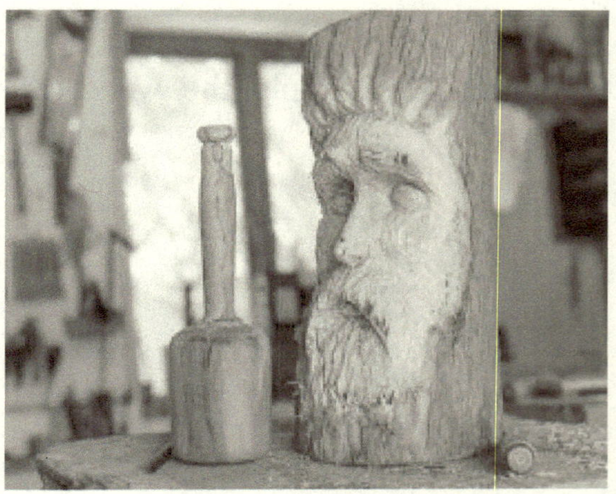

If you are looking for an easy and beginner-friendly project to get you started on whittling, you'll love this project. Not only is it easy to whittle, but it is also a fantastic decorative piece, and you can even use it as a key holder. The wood spirit is a mythical being believed to be living within trees and will one day come to life. If you are interested in carving a forest spirit, then this is how to go about it.

The Required Materials

- A whittling knife
- A pen or pencil
- A piece of wood
- A selection of gouges

- Acrylic paint

Procedure

1. Start by drawing the rough outline of the wood spirit on the piece of wood.
2. Using your whittling knife, carve along the outline you've drawn to distinguish the features clearly.
3. Use the tip of your knife to cut into and along the marked lines around the nose and eyebrows as you work your way down.
4. Carve out the eyes in layers until you reach the depth you want.
5. Clear off the wood surrounding the face to create the skin line of the face and create a smooth, clean surface.
6. Burn in the cheekbones to give your carving character.
7. Cut down the line of the beard and peel the bark off.
8. Next, peel the bark of the mustache, then you can add extra details by cutting lips under the mouth and between the mustache and beard.
9. Paint the carving as you see fit.

Chisel Carved Tiki Idol

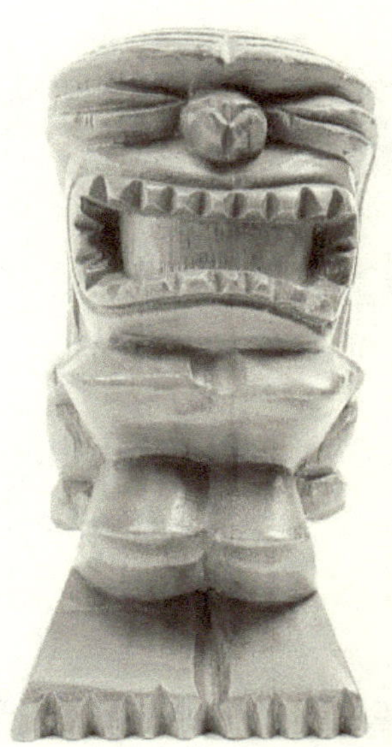

The tiki is one of the oldest carvings to be ever made, and it was used to represent a Polynesian god. Like the way Christians believe that Adam was the first created human, Maori mythology refers to tiki as the first man. Therefore, getting to carve this statue is an excellent idea because not only do you get to experience this culture, but it is also a great project for practicing your whittling skills. Here is how to whittle this iconic carving:

The Required Materials

- 45mm by 90mm wood

- Whittling knife
- A selection of gouges
- Pencil or pen
- Wood safe finish

Procedure

1. Begin by drawing the rough outline of the tiki on the piece of wood.
2. Remove the excess wood using your whittling knife around the eyes, eyebrows, and body.
3. Cut around the edges of your lines by following the lines with your whittling knife to cut the grain cleanly.
4. Burn in the details by carving in the eyes, mouth, forehead, and other key features of the body.
5. Use your whittling knife to rough out the excess wood around your carving until it is smooth and clean.
6. Once your carving has all the details carved in place, sand the whole carving until it is smooth.
7. Finally, paint the carving according to your liking.

Wooden Tobacco Pipe

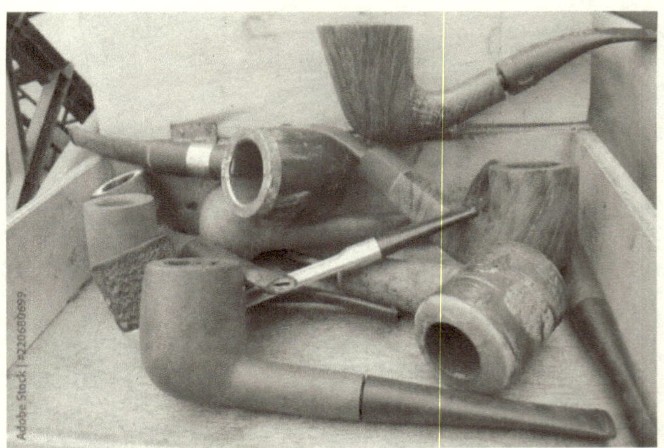

Perhaps you would want to work on something that you can actually use. If so, then a wooden tobacco pipe might be your jam- kind of like those used traditionally by pipe smokers. This project is simple and not as daunting as some of the projects detailed above.

The Required Materials

- A single piece of wood
- Belt sander for shaping
- Sandpaper
- Drill and drill bit
- Natural oil

- File
- Chisel
- Band saw

Procedure

1. Bore your bowl deep enough to hold the tobacco.
2. Ensure the bowl is evenly spaced on both sides, i.e., make sure to leave the same space on both sides of the bowl.
3. The next thing is the stem hole. Make sure your stem hole is centrally placed and not on the side. You can bore it diagonally if you wish to go for the fancier look.
4. Shape the pipe beginning with cutting off the sides of the bowl and discarding off the waste.
5. Even out the sides using the belt sander.
6. Sand the sculpture down to smooth it out.
7. You can check your piece for any leaks by covering your bowl and blowing air into the stem. If any of it escapes, you can apply glue to seal the leak as you want a functional and effective piece.

8. Coat the inside of the stem hole with natural oil. You will be consuming the tobacco, so it is advisable to keep away from any harsh chemicals, stick to natural ones.

Carved Eagle Feather

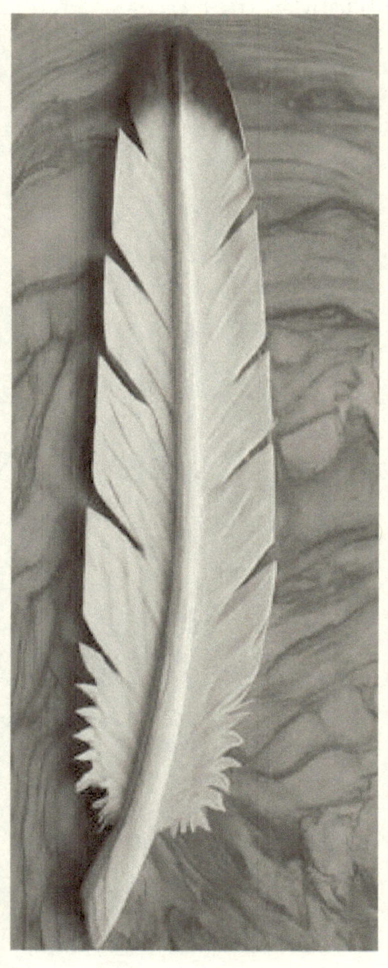

Have you been whittling for as long as you can remember and would like a project that will send you a little off-trail? Then this is the perfect project for you. A detailed eagle feather will be just the project for you to hone and sharpen your whittling skills. This fine sculpture can be very well used as wall décor, and you can brag about hand carving an outstanding piece of art when your friends come over.

The Required Materials

- A piece of wood
- Desired pattern
- Band saw
- Whittling knife
- Sandpaper
- Pencil
- Paints and brushes for that extra spice

Procedure

1. Trace the pattern on the wood and cut it out with a band saw.
2. Once done, draw in the rest of the eagle pattern lines with a pencil.
3. Thin and round off the feather. Apply extreme caution to ensure that you don't injure yourself while at it.

4. Using a V-tool, make a stop cut along the quill on both sides and make it as deep as possible.
5. Then using your knife, remove the excess wood from the feather.
6. Round off all the hard edges
7. Smooth out your sculpture by sanding, making sure there are no saw marks on it.
8. Add the lines by using a V- tool.
9. You can then paint the feather to your liking. Maybe a brown color might do.

Boomerang

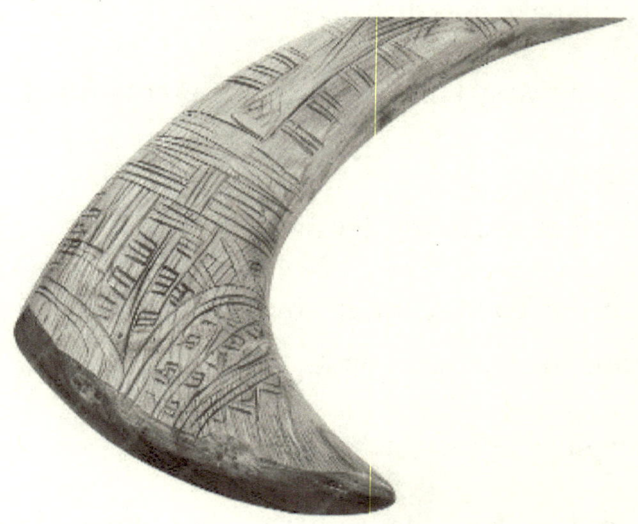

This is one of the easiest and most exciting projects you can ever try. Not only is the design easy, but it also doesn't take a lot of time to make. A boomerang would make the perfect play toy, and its interesting nature of using it will fascinate you. You can make work even easier when carving this project by finding a natural elbow wood that you can carve from. However, you can also carve it entirely from a block of wood; it is all up to you.

The Required Materials

- Grafting wax
- Pocket saw

- Vice
- Sander
- Natural oil
- Whittling knife
- Glue

Procedure

1. The first step is to find a natural elbow wood with a diameter of 10cm more or less. Make sure to pick the most curved branch because the more it's curved, the better.

2. Let the freshly cut wood dry out before you can start carving because fresh wood is not suitable for handling directly.

3. Next, plane the elbow to have a flat surface on both sides with a thickness that is almost the same everywhere.

4. Now slice the elbow into two to make it as thin as possible using a saw.

5. The next step is for you to shape your boomerang using a jigsaw, sander, and plane.

6. Profile and flatten the ends of the boomerang so that you can perform basic aerodynamics on it.
7. Finally, when your boomerang is all carved up and detailed, oil it thoroughly to give it some protection.

Carving a Willow Whistle

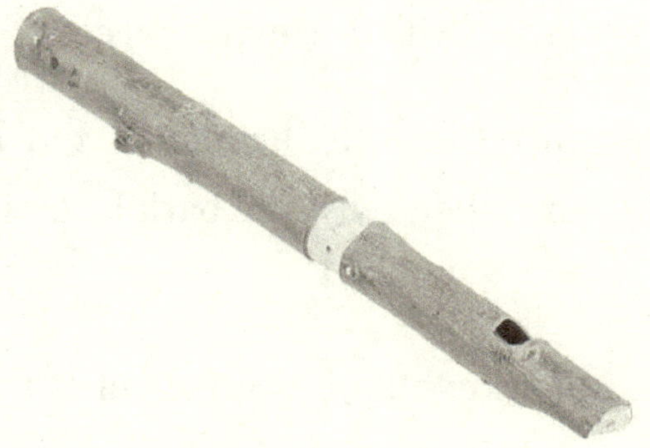

Any scout will tell you that having a whistle in the woods is essential because you can use it to signal, play a tune, or have fun with it. Therefore if you'd like an easy-to-make and fun whittling project, then this one is for you. You can easily make it using your whittling knife and a small branch you can find around.

The Required Materials

- A whittling knife
- A small piece of branch that is about 3 to 5 inches long and the diameter of your finger
- V tool
- Sandpaper

Procedure

1. Start by cutting a 45-degree bevel on one side of the stick to act as the whistle's mouthpiece.
2. Now tap the whistle with the handle of your knife to loosen the bark, then twist the bark lose until it comes off.
3. Cut off the bevel part with 90 degrees cut of the air hole to allow air to go into the whistle.
4. Put the remaining part into the other end of the bark, then remove the wood from inside the whistle.
5. Finally, you can sand your whistle or paint it as you see fit.

The Ball and Cage

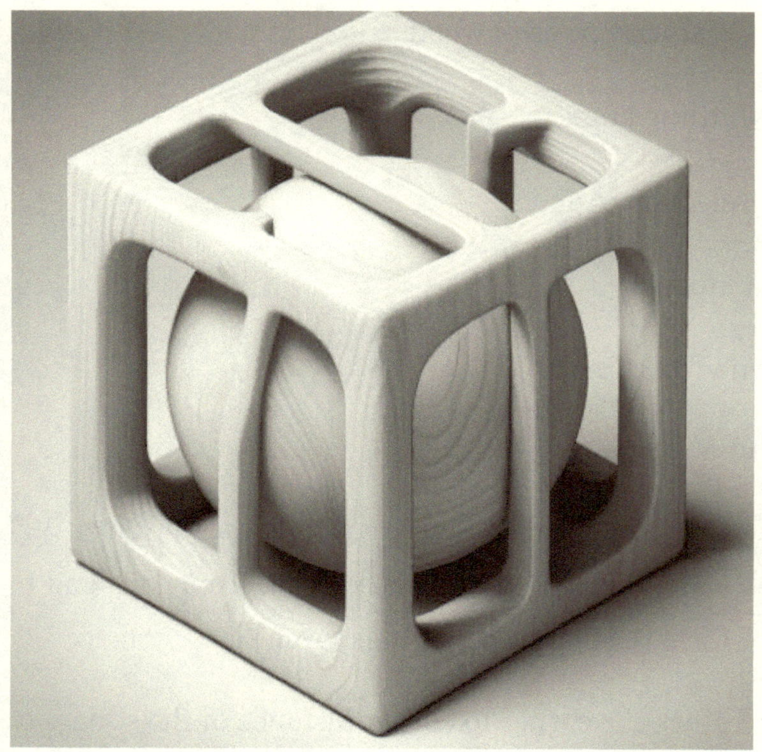

If you'd like a project that will help spice things up, then the ball and cage is a classic piece. Not only is it a great decorative piece, but it is also great for practicing your whittling skills. The best part is that you can make even longer patterns using this ball and cage design to create some type of chain. Also, there are many variations to the ball and cage depending on the number of balls you'd like to whittle and the shape you decide to pick. Here is how you are to whittle this particular project.

The Required Materials

- 1 ¼" square piece of wood
- Whittling knife
- A selection of gouges
- Sandpaper
- Wood safe finish

Procedure

1. Begin by marking the cage rails on the block ¼" wide, then go on and mark ½" in from each end to form the end pieces of the cage.

2. Mark the corner to corner distance of the square to act as the width of the ball.

3. Make deep stop cuts along each window adjacent to the ball section on all four sides. Do this in steps until there is no wood on the window sections.

4. Now make stop cuts around the ball area while you split small wedges of wood as you go until the cuts meet on each side and the block in the middle slides freely.

5. Round of the ball by making tiny cuts on all the sides until it is all round and smooth.

6. Make sure to remove all the wood around the ball while keeping in mind not to remove more wood than necessary until the ball falls off.

7. Sand the entire carving and apply the wood-safe finish.

Whittling a Flying Propeller

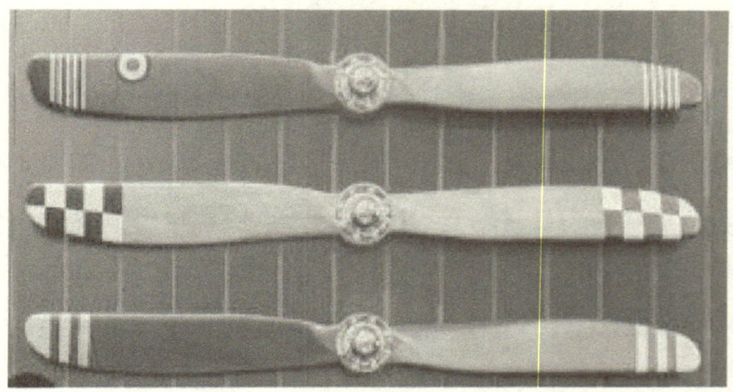

A propeller makes for a unique outdoor project, especially if you want to sculpt something quick and easy. It would also make a great gift for a kid because a propeller is a fun thing to play with.

Some people even use it as a decorative piece that rotates when blown by the wind. To fly a propeller, you need to hold the bottom of the handle against your left-hand heel with the fingers of your right hand. Now reverse the hands of your left-handed propeller, then push the right hand forward.

The Required Materials

- Whittling knife
- ½" by ½" by 9" wood
- ½" by 1 ½" by 8" wood
- Wood glue

Procedure

1. Begin by squaring up the edges of the blank down to 5/16" by 1" by 8", then mark the hole for the handle by measuring 4" from one end, making a mark ½" in from the edge.

2. Now drill the hole for the handle through the middle of the blank.

3. Next, whittle the right corner of the blank by starting about ¼" from the hole, then repeat the same procedure on the other end of the propeller.

4. Round off the sharp corners before checking if your propeller is balanced.

5. To check if your propeller is balanced correctly, line the edge of your blade up on the corner of the hole, then see if the propeller tips. If it does tip, shave wood off the heavy side a little until it balances.

6. The handle of the propeller should be about 1" longer than the propeller so that it can stabilize and help it fly. So if you have trouble flying the propeller, then make a slightly longer handle.

7. Finally, shape the handle to be round and smooth before using the wood glue to join it properly to the head of the propeller.

Carve Wooden Mini Mushrooms

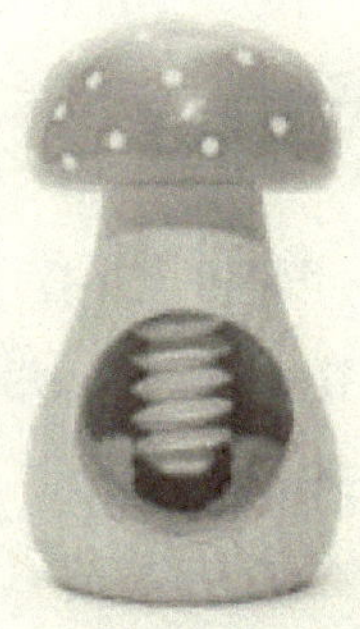

Landscaping your home can be a lot of work, and that's why you need all the ideas you can get. One way to improve the aesthetics of your home is by making these wooden mushrooms and displaying them around your home. You can do this with different colors then put them around your home. The best part is that whittling a mushroom is very easy and does not take a lot of time.

The Required Materials

- Branches of different sizes
- Your whittling knife
- Sandpaper
- Acrylic paints

Procedure

1. Start by selecting one of the sticks you'd like to start with; then, while holding one end, cut across the end to mark the top of the mushroom.

2. Using your whittling knife, start to strip away the bark around 1 cm down from the top, then using more pressure, whittle it into a rounded end.

3. Before stripping off the back, make sure to decide how long you'd like the mushroom cap to be.

4. Leave a thin strip of bark on the lower part of the cap, then, use a sharp whittling knife to create a shallow cut a few millimeters deep all around.

5. Now carve away the bark and wood to the line you made. How long the stem will be is up to you.

6. Leave a few millimeters of the bark at the base of the stem, cut the mushroom of the stick using your knife.

7. Finally, sand the carved surfaces, then paint as you'd like. Repeat the same procedure for other mushrooms.

Carving a Mini Ship

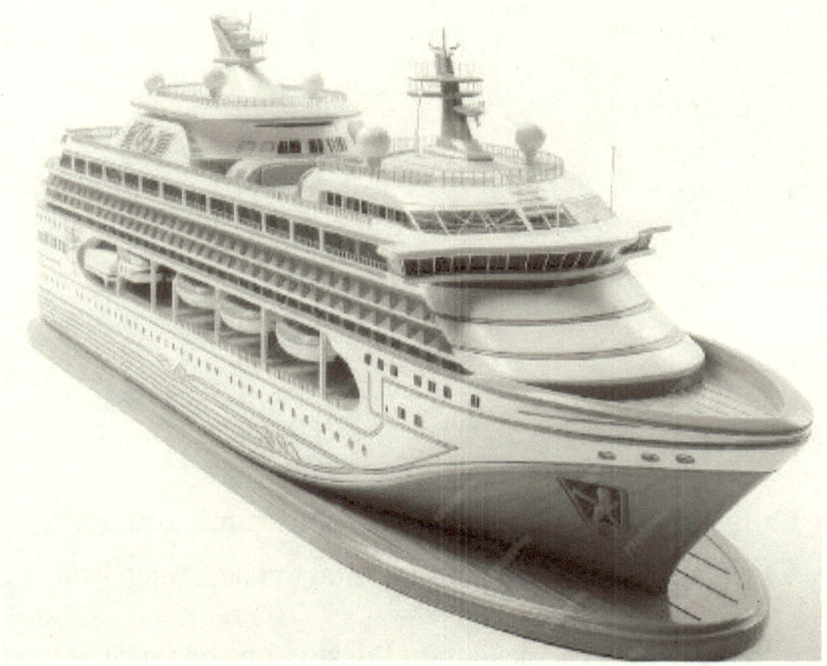

How cool will it be to make your own ship from scratch? And the best part is that it is quite easy and will not take up much of your time. Ships have been a classic since time immemorial because they bring a nice touch to a place. Therefore, this project would make for a unique decorative piece. You'll also be able to practice your whittling skills as you enhance your creativity. This is how to go about it if you decide to carve a mini ship.

The Required Materials

- Whittling knife

- A piece of wood
- Superglue
- Hammer
- Drill
- Chisel
- String

Procedure

1. Begin by shaving down your stick until you get down to the actual wood if you decide to use a thick branch.
2. Draw the basic design on the ship on the piece of wood using a pencil, then start carving using your whittling knife.
3. Now make sure that the top and bottom parts of the ship are as parallel as possible by carving them as flat as you can.
4. Next, draw out the top, back, and bottom of the ship, then carve them out the same way you did to the top and bottom. Again, make sure to keep it as flat as possible.

5. Carve out the inside of your ship using the chisel as deep as you'd like your boat to be.

6. Drill the holes and make some masts that will go with the skewers.

7. Shave down a small part of the skewer to make it nice and pokey at the tip.

8. Decide the number of sails you need, then using a cloth and the sticks, make some for your ship.

9. Attach the sails to your ship and many as you want or as tall as you'd like, then use glue to attach them to the ship.

10. Sand the whole ship and apply the wood-safe finish.

Whittling a Boat

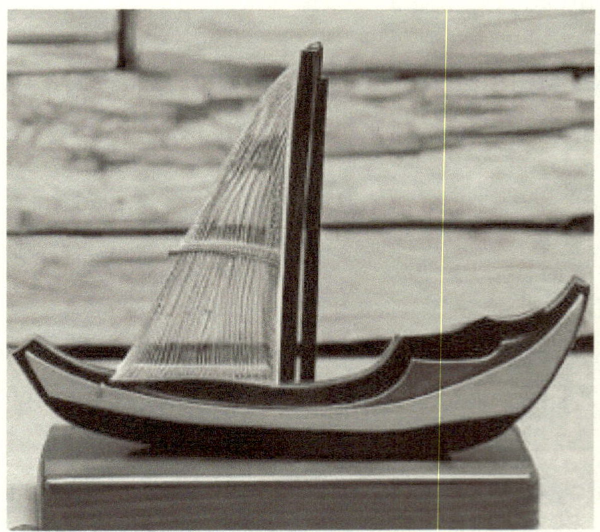

Have you always been a water lover and loved how a boat is just the perfect way to find your way in water? If so, then dive right into this project and explore your love for boats. A boat can serve as a great office desk décor. The interesting bit is that it is effortless to make one. When you accomplish this sculpture, you'll feel a deep sense of satisfaction and pride in a job well done. You can even challenge yourself to make a real wooden boat once you excel in this whittling project.

The Required Materials

- Softwood
- A sharp whittling knife

- Oilstone
- Band saw
- Flat blade
- Digging blade

Procedure

1. Trace the required pattern of the boat on thin tissue paper.
2. Find the correct size of wood that will fit the pattern.
3. Trace the pattern of the boat on the wood.
4. Cut the woodblock to the pattern shape using a band saw to avoid causing wear and tear on the knife.
5. Shape the exterior of the boat. Flatten the bottom of the hull.
6. Use a flat blade to carve the inside of the boat.
7. Hollow out the interior. Using your digging blade, shape the inside of the boat.
8. It's now time for the more refined finishing. Make some final touches to fine-tune your design. Smooth

out your boat, and voila! There you have your whittled boat.

Conclusion

Like any other skill, becoming a pro whittler requires a lot of practice. Even though it might be challenging at the beginning, once you have all the necessary tools and information, you'll be able to whittle any project you like. Just try all the projects listed in this book, and by the time you are finished with the last one, you'll have become a seasoned whittler.

All the best!

www.ingramcontent.com/pod-product-compliance
Lightning Source LLC
LaVergne TN
LVHW051003080826
845145LV00009B/2435

* 9 7 8 1 9 5 1 7 3 7 8 1 8 *